WORK H
PLAYLIST HARD

SECOND EDITION

WRITTEN BY
MIKE WARNER

Disclaimers

The information in this book is based on the author's personal experiences. It does not constitute advice or a recommendation of any product or service. Neither the author nor publisher accepts any responsibility for any errors, omissions or inaccuracy in the information or for any loss or damage that may result from usage of this material.

Information provided by contributors within this book is shared from their own experiences and written in their own words.

All screenshots were captured on the author's computer or mobile device while logged into their own account unless indicated otherwise.

Introduction

This book shares everything I wish I knew when I started out. It also details vital parts of my journey, from a keen music lover and starving music producer to a successful streaming music nerd who makes a living in this beautiful, crazy industry. It is the result of many conversations with friends, artists, labels and managers. I suggest grabbing a pen and paper.

I've been a music lover my entire life, with a music collection of funk, hip hop, punk, rock, electronic, ska and everything in between. I spent 20 years DJing, hosted multiple podcasts and radio shows, helped numerous artists transition to becoming independent, produced music under various aliases and worked with a few background music services. After many years of trying to break into the music industry, applying to multiple jobs, I concluded that my resume wasn't strong enough.

I decided to build my own opportunities through self education. What I've learned is that artists today have more power, tools and opportunity than ever before. They just need to be given the right knowledge to succeed.

Many pieces of advice I share are inspired by a question from an artist. This book is written as though I am telling you how to set up an artist for success through the use of streaming services, all while building value in their brand through strong playlist curation. These insights are for artists, managers, label reps or any of many new roles in the music industry.

This second edition is no longer just focused on playlist pitching and curation. It has grown into so much more than that. It's packed full of tools and features that are available to help an artist get their music in front of a wider audience and provide them with strategies for long-term growth across many platforms.

That being said, sections of the book will still be similar to the first edition with its focus on playlists and curation. In addition, you'll see a focus on online presence, data, tools and all of the things that can help an artist to grow.

Without further ado, welcome to *Work Hard Playlist Hard,* the second edition. Here we go!

TIP: WHEN YOU SEE TEXT LABELED "TIP" LIKE THIS, PAY CLOSE ATTENTION. THESE ARE SHORT, QUICK, PIECES OF GOLD.

What is a Playlist?

A playlist is a list of songs that can be listened to through a DSP. The playlist can be listened to either sequentially or in a shuffled order.

DSP MEANS "DIGITAL SERVICE PROVIDER". A DSP CAN BE A RETAIL STORE LIKE ITUNES OR A MUSIC STREAMING PROVIDER SUCH AS SPOTIFY, APPLE MUSIC OR DEEZER.

Playlists have existed for many years in many mediums, from cassette tapes to radio, but we will be exclusively referring to playlists on DSPs.

Playlists can help a new audience to discover your music through association. Similar to changing stations on your TV or radio stations in your car, playlists offer a variety of music from both independent and label artists.

Over 75,000 songs are added to a DSP every single day in the United States alone. Let that sink in for a second! Playlists help you stand out from all of the other songs. Think of them as a public showcase of music with uncapped potential reach. Artists have found themselves being able to create major tours, sign lucrative record deals, gain placement in films and television shows and even quit their day jobs. These and many other stories are becoming more common as artists find a way to monetize their craft and be strategic with playlist pitching to ensure their music reaches as many ears as possible.

There are countless types of playlists out there. Each playlist has a different kind of value and method required.

Editorial Playlists

Editorial playlists are curated by staff who work directly for the streaming platform. These can provide significant streaming numbers but should not be your only goal as these curators rarely communicate with artists and their support is never guaranteed. While some of these editorial curators don't have a strong online presence, there are a few exceptions.

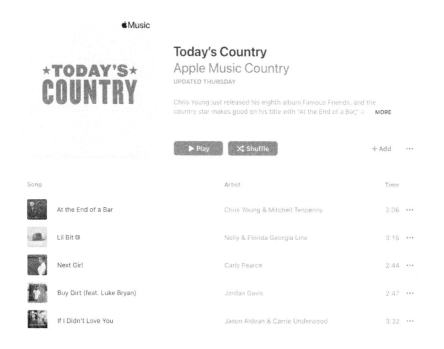

How Can I Find An Editorial Playlist?

Editorial playlists are easily identified because the curator/user name matches the DSP. Spotify, for example, will show "Created by Spotify" on each playlist that they own.

As an exercise, take a look at the following editorial playlists. Ideally you should follow playlists that you would like to see your music placed on. This helps you get a better understanding of what the editors are looking for.

Amazon Music

All Hits

Country Heat

Pop Culture

Apple Music

danceXL

New Music Daily

Today's Hits

Deezer

Acoustic Pop

Deezer Hits

Urban Hits

Spotify

Beast Mode

Mint

Peaceful Piano

Today's Top Hits

YouTube Music

Alternative Hotlist

<u>Highline R&B</u>

<u>Pop Hotlist</u>

Who Are These Editorial Curators?

While most editorial curators fly under the radar and prefer to remain a mystery, there are a few that are active on social media. Follow them and familiarize yourself with what they are looking for. Then, when the time is right, make your move.

User-Generated Playlists

Also known as "third party playlists", these are curated by regular users like yourself who make their playlists public for anyone to follow and stream. By making a connection with the owners of these playlists, you may have a better chance of receiving future support from them.

One benefit of user-generated playlists is that you have an opportunity to find that user and connect with them through social media, email, or other means. They are usually a lot more accessible than editorial curators.

How Can I Find A User Playlist?

If you look at the "Created By" section under the description you will see a name. Click on that name and it will take you to their profile. You will clearly see the word "user" on their profile.

Screenshot: User profile on Spotify.

How Do I Contact The Curator?

Here are a few strategies to try and locate playlist owners. Of course, these are only suggestions and may not work for every person. (This first one is a sneaky tactic I've found that works in some instances.)

Google Image Search

Google allows you to take a screenshot of the user's profile picture, then upload it to Google and search for matching instances of that image. If the photo is a unique photo of the person, you may find links to their social media or website in the search results. People tend to use the same profile picture across all social media.

Visit https://images.google.com to use this feature.

Facebook

Spotify allows users to sign in with their Facebook credentials, which also uses their current Facebook profile photo and name on their Spotify profile. A quick Facebook search can often match the name and photo to the user profile in Spotify.

Chartmetric

Chartmetric has data for millions of playlists across various DSPs. When possible, the website and social media URLs for the curator will be listed. This can be useful when trying to find a way to contact the curator through social media.

Brand Playlists

Many brands have utilized playlists to reach their customers outside of their stores. Brand playlists keep customers connected and offer some nice benefits in the way of free advertising. For example, Nike has running playlists, Disney has singalong playlists, Starbucks has a latte playlists (See what I did there?).

Celebrities or influencers can also be verified with a brand account. These are usually very hard to contact without having a direct contact the management company.

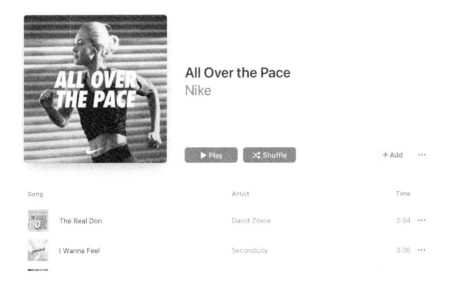

Song	Artist	Time
The Real Don	David Zowie	2:54 •••
I Wanna Feel	Secondcity	3:06 •••

Who runs these brand playlists?

Usually, someone on the marketing team is in charge of curation. However, there are some companies that have a music department which oversees live performances, music for tv commercials and playlists. The best way to find a lead is by doing a quick internet search. There's often at least one blog post that spotlights their curators.

Background Music Services

Ask your parents (or maybe even grandparents) what MUZAK is, and you may be surprised. This is not a new thing. Background music ("in-store" or "overhead" music) has been around for many years. Fortunately, music has evolved from "elevator music" to feature various music from independent to established artists.

This is free money, as I like to say. Most background music services will only add music that is directly licensed to them, meaning the only way to get your music played in stores they service - and to get paid for that play - is to license your music to them. This doesn't mean that they own your music. It means they have your permission to use it. Of course, always read the contract.

Imagine shopping in Macy's, hearing your song blasting through the speakers and seeing someone whip out their phone to Shazam it. This additional exposure can lead to a growing fanbase on Apple Music and Spotify. Shazam now even allows users to directly stream songs previously Shazamed, in full. This counts as a play, and you can even add your "My Shazamed Tracks" playlist on both service.

To get you started, I have listed a selection of background music services that have previously accepted submissions from me. Reach out via their general email on their website, first asking for their music submission process. Once you have the correct contact information, follow up with your most recent single only. If they like your latest release and want your whole back catalog of music, they will ask you. Don't send everything in the first email.

Mood Media (Global)

Nightlife Music (Australia and New Zealand)

PlayNetwork (USA)

RX Music (USA/Canada)

SoundMachine

Soundtrack Your Brand (Global)

Stingray Music (Canada and Australia)

StorePlay (Australia)

Tastemaker Playlists

These are much more rare to see. In Spotify, when you go to a user's profile, instead of saying "user" near their profile photo it will say "tastemaker". Rumor has it Tastemakers have earned this status through solid curation.

Why are Tastemakers so valuable?

Spotify doesn't go into great detail about tastemakers, but it's believed that if a tastemaker places a song, this could contribute towards a song's placement across various editorial playlists.

Where can I find Tastemakers?

Spotify used to showcase Tastemakers in the **Browse** section of the app. There used to be a section called **Who To Follow** that suggested friends and other curators, but this has since been removed. The only current way is simply to ask around and look at the profile page for every user. If you see "Tastemaker", copy the URL and add it to a spreadsheet. Start keeping track of these as you come across them.

Algorithmic Playlists

Curated by robots, fed by metadata, these playlists deliver different music to each user based on their listening habits and taste. These playlists include Release Radar, Discover Weekly and Your Daily Mix on Spotify.

One of the best ways to make sure that your music has every opportunity to be heard on these playlists is by adding as much detail as possible. When filling out Editorial submission forms and uploading music through a distributor be sure to always include as much detail as possible.

Personalized Editorial

These playlists are curated by staff, but playlist songs and order are customized for each listener. For example, if you and someone next to you both open Spotify and follow "Weekend Hangouts", the playlist will be different for each of you.

This is because Spotify creates a pool of up to 600 songs that are available for each personalized editorial playlist depending on the listener. Each listener's playlist is then capped at around 100 songs, resulting in a very different and personalized experience for each individual listener. The good thing about these playlists is that there are more opportunities for more artists to get heard from them because the bank of music is larger.

Distributor Playlists

House Music 2021 | Dance Anthems

 Topsify

The hottest dance tracks, updated every week!
84 tracks · 3 hrs 58 mins · 19,422 fans · Updated: 1 week ago

LISTEN   ♡ ↪ ···   MANUAL ⌄   Search in the Playlist

#		TRACK		ARTIST	L.	POP.	
1	♡	The Business		Tiësto	02:44	‖‖‖‖	
2	♡	Heartbreak Anthem		Galantis, David Guetta...	03:03	‖‖‖‖	
3	♡	Oh My		Parx	03:00	‖‖‖‖	
4	♡	Nirvana		A7S	02:37	‖‖‖‖	

It's not uncommon for record labels and distributors to also curate their own playlists. Here are a few examples:

- <u>Topsify</u>
- <u>Filtr</u>
- <u>Digster</u>

Other distributors also curate under their own names:

- CD Baby
- Ditto
- DistroKid
- TuneCore

Artist Playlists

Artist playlists can grow very quickly with the right network of supportive fans. These are extremely valuable as the artist has full control over the music that is featured.

It's not uncommon for artists that are no longer creating new music to still have well maintained playlists. These playlists will always be a home for fans to enjoy their music. Plus, if the playlist has a significant following it is highly valuable to the artist's manager/label who can then include songs from similar artists in the playlist to give them a boost.

Update Your Playlist Regularly

Contributed by Nina Las Vegas

When promoting my own artist playlist on Spotify, I've found that consistency is key. People return to your playlist if they know you update it regularly. As someone who follows a lot of playlists to find new music, I know I get annoyed when they're barely refreshed, so I try to keep that mentality when working on my own!

My "Track IDs" playlist is updated every two weeks, and I make sure to promote it across as many platforms as possible. Every two weeks, I do a little drawing, something that my followers have become familiar with since Instagram started. I always tag the smaller, emerging artists in my post when I share, as those are the people that are more excited to share their placements. These days, with TikTok also driving a lot of playlisting awareness, I film myself drawing each little promo tile and post that on the platform.

Nina's Track ID's playlist can be found on Spotify

Find out more about Nina at ninalasvegas.com

Podcast and Blog Playlists

Contributed by Bree Noble

Many podcasts and blogs, especially if they are based on a particular theme, curate playlists from the songs they feature.

As the founder of the *Women of Substance* music podcast (wosradio.com), I produce several themed podcast episodes each year that I curate into playlists.

Some examples include the Love Songs For Valentines series, the Music With A Conscience series and my Holiday series. Since the podcast is already curated with high quality music around a very specific theme, combining the songs from the series into a playlist is a perfect fit.

I don't just promote the playlists through my own channels. I get all the artists onboard promoting it to their fans, asking them to like, listen and share because it benefits everyone.

So, when submitting music to a podcast or blog, search Spotify to see if that platform also creates playlists. These are very worthwhile opportunities to pursue because they offer a double dose of exposure.

Find out more about Bree at breenoble.com

Let's Get Social

If you haven't already, sign up for the following social media accounts. If you are against social media, it's time to suck it up and accept that for many people in this industry it is the fastest way to make initial contact, forge a friendship, find your fans and continue the relationship when they stop streaming. Here are five platforms you should, at the very least, claim a username on.

- Facebook
- Twitter
- LinkedIn
- Instagram
- TikTok

Use the same username for all services. This is important for consistency and helping people find you. If you are @JSmithTunes on Instagram, then your Twitter handle should be @JSmithTunes. Make it easy for fans from your other platforms to tweet, mention or follow you.

To keep it consistent, do a quick check on all social media sites before locking into your username. For example, go to facebook.com/jsmithtunes, instagram.com/jsmithtunes etc. to see if the username is available. You can do this from a web browser much more quickly than by searching in the apps.

TIP: HERE'S A SITE YOU CAN USE TO CHECK ALL SOCIALS AT THE SAME TIME - CHECKUSERNAMES.COM. IF ANY NEW SOCIAL MEDIA APPS OR SITES LAUNCH AFTER THIS BOOK IS RELEASED PLEASE ALSO SIGN UP FOR THOSE, EVEN IF IT IS JUST TO CLAIM YOUR UNIQUE USERNAME. IF A NEW SOCIAL MEDIA PLATFORM TAKES OFF, YOU WANT TO HAVE YOUR HANDLE LOCKED IN, JUST IN CASE!

Of course, I'm not just going to tell you to sign up and then "get to work". Below are tips on creating a good social media profile and where and how to find your first contacts. Once you've found them, don't do anything yet. Write them down on that piece of paper I had you grab.

GOLDEN RULES WHEN CREATING PROFILES ON SOCIAL MEDIA:

- Give professional information and use a name you're serious about. Your real name or artist name should be what you lead with on your public pages.

- Use a real photo of your face. Show that you are a real person. Don't post crowd shots or a picture of the back of your head staring into the sunset.

- Don't use fake credentials. Don't undersell yourself either. If you have been producing music for two weeks, don't include that in your bio. You can try something else like "Music Producer, Australia". If people want to know more, they will ask you.

It's important to let your audience know which platforms you are most active on. That way if they use multiple social media platforms they know which one they are going to see the most content from you on. As an author and executive, I post most frequently on LinkedIn. That's the platform where I spend most of my time on, and that's the one I promote first. Artists may find themselves more frequently on Instagram, Twitch or Twitter.

Put some thought into what kinds of posts you put on each platform. For example, behind-the-scenes studio photos are best on Instagram, quick spontaneous thoughts work great for Twitter and achievements and professional developments are most appropriate for LinkedIn.

Make a Plan and Grind It Out

Contributed by Troy Carter Jr.

My advice to artists all across the globe would be to set an intention. Set intent for your career, outline the direction you want to go in and get everybody on your team on the same page. Walk, run or fly in that direction, but have a direction.

The game is more competitive than it's ever been. Ultimately, you have to be intentional with everything that you're doing. This includes:

- The music you are releasing

- The time you release it

- When your music videos are coming out

- What you're posting on social media

I think there's an underlying myth that you just kind of "make it", which is never the case. Anybody you see that is very successful today got there through a very deliberate plan of action.

Even though releases may seem spontaneous, they aren't. They are extremely calculated and artists at every level have to adapt to the climate of the industry we're in.

My advice is to set some intent. Write a plan and then grind it out. Good luck to everybody reading, I'm doing the same thing.

Find out more about Troy at <u>diamondent.org</u>

Record Labels Vs. Distributors

Contributed by Jay Gilbert

People often refer to "major labels" when they mean major music groups and/or major distributors.

Distributor examples: Ingrooves, The Orchard, Symphonic, DistroKid

Label examples: Atlantic, Sub Pop, New West, Nonesuch

The terms "label" and "distributor" are frequently used interchangeably. The truth is, they are completely different animals with very little overlap of roles and responsibilities. Let's look at the differences:

Generally speaking, **distributors** typically handle:

- Global digital distribution and monetization

- Physical and digital product release coordination

- Best practices and troubleshooting across DSPs and social platforms

- Surface insights and analytics on release performance

- Pitching to DSPs for playlists and marketing programs

- Content ID and channel optimization on YouTube

- Social media verifications

- Rights management

- Pitching for syncs (potentially)

- Pseudo videos (cover image + audio bed)

Generally speaking, **labels** typically handle:

- Release strategy / marketing plan
- Radio
- Photography
- Sync licensing
- Placing Advertising
- Full digital marketing strategy
- Online assets
- Music videos / lyric videos
- Events (except in-stores)

Find out more about Jay at label-logic.net

Artist Profiles and DSP Tools

Even if you only have one song released, this is crucial. It's essential to have a profile with as much information as possible. If your song gets in front of the editorial team at a major streaming service, your artist profile is the first thing they'll see. If you have a photo, brief biography and an artist playlist, you'll be well ahead of other artists who don't.

In the first edition of this book I shared direct links to artist portals on each DSP and urged you to sign up. Since then, the amount of tools that are provided for artists have gone far beyond simply the ability to upload a profile photo and a bio. A lot of DSPs are also providing a suite of marketing tools that can be used.

The best part is that most of these tools are provided absolutely free. As such, something that was once just one chapter is now going to be a significant portion of this book. I highly suggest creating a quick checklist as we go to make sure that you have claimed your artist profile on each platform and are aware of all the tools and features they offer.

Please be aware that not every streaming platform and tool will be covered in this book. These are the platforms I have had experience using and feel comfortable sharing. (It's also worth noting since the previous edition, Google Play has now been shut down and replaced by YouTube Music.)

Requesting access to Spotify for Artists was quite a challenge initially. Artists would need a minimum of 250 followers on Spotify and would have to answer a series of questions, then wait 4+ weeks hoping for a response. Fortunately this process has become much quicker and various music distributors offer a way to get access almost instantly. Let's go through the steps here.

- Visit artists.spotify.com and click **Get Access**.

- On the next screen click **Continue**.

- Type the artist name, or paste the artist's Spotify link into the search box. Click on the artist name from the search results.

- On the next screen, you will see one of two options:

Option 1: If your distributor has a connection with Spotify, they will have a way for you to fast-track the verification process. This can save you lots of waiting time and sometimes give instant access. If presented with this option, take it!

Option 2. Login with your Spotify account (free or premium) and continue the manual verification process.

After following the above steps, you will either receive instant verification or an email detailing when you can expect to receive access.

Spotify Artist Profile

Profile and Banner Photo

Profile and banner photos capture people's attention when they view your profile. It shows that you have taken the time to update your profile and make this into a home for your fans.

Avoid text and logos in your photo. Keep in mind parts of the photos will be cropped, so there may be some trial and error with uploading different images to find your perfect fit. We had to upload a few different photos before finding one where our faces can all be seen.

About

In this section, you can add multiple photos, a bio, and social media links.

Image Gallery

Uploading photos to the Image Gallery is extremely important. By uploading, you are giving Spotify permission to use these images in various marketing communications such as Release Radar, New Release Announcements and upcoming "shows in your city" emails. Spotify can only use an image if you have uploaded one in your profile. It can lead to some awesome free marketing, so upload those photos!

We have seen our images used in email blasts from Spotify announcing upcoming concerts and shows as well as emails sharing New Releases for the week.

Bio

A biography tells your story and helps new fans to learn a little more about you and your music.

TIP: WHILE EDITING YOUR BIO, YOU CAN TYPE @ AND LINK TO ANY OTHER ARTIST, PLAYLIST, SONG OR ALBUM ON SPOTIFY. CAN'T FIND THE RIGHT ARTIST IN THE SEARCH RESULTS? YOU CAN TYPE @ AND PASTE THE SPOTIFY URI OR URL DIRECTLY AFTER TO MAKE SURE YOU LINK TO THE CORRECT SOURCE:

Artist's Pick

The Artist's Pick feature allows you to showcase a song, album, podcast, playlist, fundraiser or concert at the top of your artist profile. This is a great way to promote a new single or playlist. Each pick expires after 14 days, so make a note in your calendar to update these every two weeks.

TIP: IT'S RUMORED SPOTIFY SEE WHAT ARTISTS HAVE SET AS THEIR ARTIST'S PICK. PERHAPS FEATURE AN EDITORIAL PLAYLIST YOU'VE GOT YOUR EYE TO GET THEIR ATTENTION, OR AS A WAY TO PUBLICLY SAY THANK YOU TO A CURATOR.

More Info

This is where you can link fans to your social media where they can also follow you and learn more about you. As a listener, when I find a new artist I like on Spotify, I often follow them. Then I click through to their social media and follow them there as well. This is another way to capture new fans and continue to engage with them on other platforms.

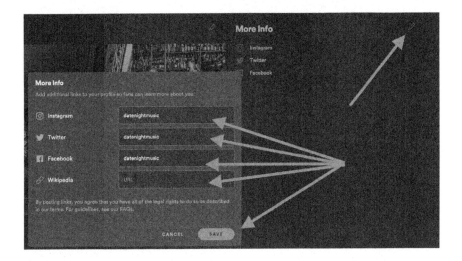

Spotify Promo Cards

This allows you to create a quick custom graphic to share on social media. You can share a milestone (e.g. 25,000 followers) or a new song, even a podcast episode.

You can change the color and size to square, portrait or landscape. You will also receive a link that you can share. While there is no current indication these links are tracked, it's safe to assume you may be able to see how many people click your customized share links in future.

This tool is available at promocards.byspotify.com

You can now create milestone cards for reaching 1k, 5k, 10k, 25k, 50k, 100k, 500k, 1M, 2M, 5M, or 10M followers on Spotify.

You can also create these for chart milestones, new release badges, live shows and dozens of eligible playlists.

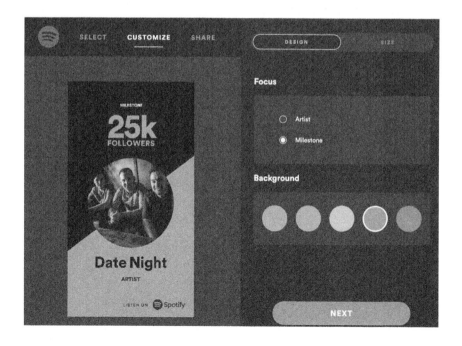

Spotify Canvas

Spotify has a cool feature called Canvas. These are 8 second vertical video loops (or visuals) that show when a song is playing. You can see these in the "Now Playing" view, in the Spotify mobile app. As of February 2021, all artists can now create a Canvas for songs through Spotify for Artists on the web or phone app. Spotify even has a Canvas designer category on their SoundBetter platform which helps artists find a designer to create a Canvas for them. Create yours at canvas.spotify.com.

Spotify and SongKick

Spotify has an integration with SongKick which allows artists to list their shows and livestreams via the On Tour tab of their Spotify profile.

Concerts and livestreams can be added to SongKick using the SongKick Toolbox which can be found at tourbox.songkick.com/artists

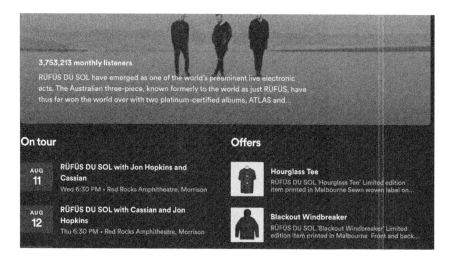

Livestreams are not instantly added and need to be approved by the SongKick team before they will appear. This can take a few days, so make sure to list these as early as possible.

SongKick can be connected by logging in to Spotify for Artists and going to **Profile,** then **Concerts**.

Once concerts are displaying correctly on an artist profile, they can also be highlighted as the Artist Pick at the top of the artist profile.

Spotify Lyric Search

Did you know you can search for a song in Spotify by entering some of its lyrics?

Let's say a fan heard a song on the radio or in a TikTok post. If they didn't catch the name, they can type in some of the lyrics they remember. For example: if I heard a song with the words "little blue balloon" I could enter it into the search bar and get results for songs that include those lyrics.

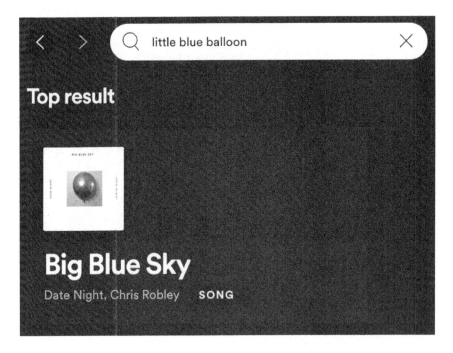

Spotify Lyrics Search is powered by MusixMatch. If you have an artist profile on Musixmatch, you'll be able to upload/deliver the lyrics to Spotify and have them indexed/searchable on Spotify. This is extremely valuable for discovery as it presents another way fans can find your music.

Lyric Search is different from synced lyrics, which scroll to show lyrics in time with the song, similar to karaoke.

Spotify Artist Playlists

Spotify allows you to feature any playlist on an artist page under the Artist Playlists section. While there is no way to curate a playlist using your public artist profile, you can curate a playlist from your regular Spotify account as a user, make it public and feature that on an artist profile.

Some artists use this section to also highlight playlists their music has been supported on and playlists they would like to see their music featured on in the future.

How to add artist playlists using your computer:

1. Log in to Spotify for Artists on your desktop.

2. Go to **Profile** and scroll down to **Artist Playlists** and click the + button.

3. Type the name of the playlist or paste the Spotify URL into the search box. Click on the playlist name to add it. Repeat this step to add multiple playlists.

4. Re-arrange the order of the Artist Playlists by clicking and dragging.

5. Click **Save**.

How to add artist playlists on your phone

1. Log in to the Spotify for Artists app on your phone.

2. Tap the profile icon (person with music note) and scroll down to **Artist Playlists** then tap on **Edit**.

3. Tap on **Add Playlist.**

4. Type the name of the playlist into the search box. Tap on the playlist name to add it. Repeat this step to add multiple playlists.

5. Re-arrange the order of the Artist Playlists by pressing your finger down and holding it to drag the playlists around.

6. Click **Save** once you're happy with the order.

7. Visit the artist profile in the Spotify app and scroll down to the bottom to see the **Artist Playlists** section.

TIP: IN THE SPOTIFY MOBILE APP YOU CAN EDIT YOUR USERNAME (WHICH SHOWS UP ON PLAYLISTS YOU CURATE). TAP "EDIT PROFILE" AND YOU CAN THEN EDIT YOUR USERNAME AND PROFILE PHOTO. CURRENTLY, YOU CAN ONLY EDIT YOUR USERNAME IN THE MOBILE APP.

Spotify Editorial Playlist Pitching

Spotify submission forms were floating around the web for a few years. For the fortunate few artists that located these mysterious Google forms, the links were closely guarded and rarely shared. With major labels and distributors able to pitch priority releases to the Spotify editorial team through other means, many independent artists expressed their feelings of being left out in the cold. Now, all users of Spotify for Artists have the opportunity to submit a song to the relevant editorial team.

If you have an upcoming release (a song that has been uploaded via a distributor but is not out yet), you will see an option at the top of your Spotify for Artists dashboard allowing you to submit a song. If your upcoming release is an album, you will only be able to submit one song from the album. Click **Pitch From Next Release** to get started.

Home

II.ı 0 people listening now

Pitch a song to our editors

Batu releases on Jun 4, 2020. Pitch a song so our playlist editors can hear it first.

PITCH FROM NEXT RELEASE →

You can also find eligible songs by navigating to the **Music** tab and then clicking **Upcoming**. From here, you can click **Pitch a Song**.

Once you submit a song, Spotify will ask you to add details relating to genre and sub genre. You can also share mood, moment, and even the location associated with your release.

In the submission form, it's important to add as much detail as possible. This information is attached to your song and will help it to be delivered to the right audience. For instance, if you create beautiful instrumental piano music, you want to make sure it reaches the classical editorial team. Correct information means your song will be delivered to various listeners through editorial and algorithmic playlists and artist radio stations in Spotify.

In the next screen, you can add a city. While this can be your hometown, it's best to choose the city where your music has the strongest cultural connection, even if it's not your hometown or current city. You can also describe your song for Spotify using 500 characters or less. This is where you tell a compelling and short story about the song. If you don't have a marketing budget, there's no need to mention it. If you can't craft a good, short story about your song, play it to someone who hasn't heard it before and ask them to describe it in a few sentences.

TIP: SPOTIFY HAS ALSO RELEASED A LARGE NUMBER OF ADDITIONAL GENRES TO CHOOSE FROM WHEN SUBMITTING MUSIC. PREVIOUSLY, ARTISTS WITH A NICHE GENRE FOUND IT TOUGH TO FIND AN EXACT MATCH WHEN SUBMITTING. WHILE THERE IS CURRENTLY A MIND-BLOWING 5,521 GENRE-SHAPED DISTINCTIONS ON SPOTIFY AT TIME OF WRITING, NOT ALL WILL BE AVAILABLE ON THE SUBMISSION FORM. YOU CAN FIND MOST OF THESE GENRES AT EVERYNOISE.COM

I have included an example from a successful pitch below. In this case, I am terrible with words so I asked the featured singer/songwriter to write something compelling.

LOVE, JUST LIKE THE PHONE ON WHICH IT'S OFTEN SPARKED, SEEMS TO FALL PREY TO PLANNED OBSOLESCENCE. LONG AFTER THE CLUB LIGHTS COOL, AFTER ALL THE SWEATY CLOTHES COME OFF, AFTER A DOZEN BROKEN HEARTS AND A HUNDRED BAD DECISIONS, YOU WOULDN'T FAULT A PERSON THESE DAYS FOR THEIR SUSPICION OF COMMITMENT. THEN AGAIN, THAT MIGHT ALSO BE THE MOMENT SOMEONE'S FINALLY READY.

It is safe to say that pitch was well received, as the song ended up on two massive editorial playlists.

Pop Chillout

Weekend Hangouts

Spotify Release Radar Reach

One very important piece of information that is often overlooked is that your song will be added into the Release Radar for ALL of your followers if you submit it at least 7 business days before release day.

Here's what's great about this. If you have 5,000 followers, that equals 5,000 Release Radar playlists that your song will be added to that week. If you've submitted for playlist consideration at least 7 days in advance, your track will automatically be shared to your followers' Release Radar playlist on release day.

Songs that are submitted fewer than 7 days in advance are not guaranteed placement on Release Radar. It's also worth noting that if you do a separate release for a remix of your song, it is not guaranteed Release Radar placement. Only original songs uploaded for the first time are guaranteed.

Spotify Marquee Campaigns

Spotify Marquee allows artists to create a full-screen sponsored recommendation for new releases. The Marquee will display in the app with a prompt to listen to the new album release.

A Marquee can be scheduled up to 18 days after a song has been released.

At time of writing, Marquee is not available in all countries and there are some minimum requirements that have to be met to be eligible.

‒ Artists must have more than 15k streams over the last 28 days in the US

‒ Marquee can only be created for new releases

‒ If promoting an album, 50% or more of the songs must be new and never previously released

‒ The artist's distributor must have enabled Marquee

To see if a Marquee can be created, login to Spotify for Artists. **Campaigns** will be visible along the top menu.

Please note that Marquee is a paid option for artists that want to promote their music directly within the Spotify app.

Spotify for Artists Stats

Spotify for Artists has a great amount of detail for where the streams and listeners from your music come from. You can see the location of those listeners, which playlists the streams come from and if people are listening directly from your artist profile.

While it can be addictive to open the app and check your stats several times a day, keep in mind that these numbers only update once every 24 hours at roughly 3pm EST.

The only exception here is in the Spotify for Artists app. Immediately after a new song is released, the live stream count shows for the first 7 days and updates every 2 seconds to show the total number of streams.

TIP: SOME ARTISTS HAVE FOUND A WAY TO INCORPORATE THIS COUNT INTO A LIVE STREAM ON SOCIAL MEDIA. IT'S A FUN WAY TO GET YOUR AUDIENCE EXCITED BY SHARING UPDATES WITH THEM.

Spotify Fan Engagement

Contributed by Mark Tavern

Improving your marketing means understanding each DSP's ecosystem and implementing strategies and tactics designed for how the platform works. With Spotify, this means better understanding its AI - specifically its algorithmic playlisting and recommendations - and tailoring your marketing to put the platform to work for you.

Marketers often talk about "push" and "pull". These are general terms that describe how marketing messages are sent and received. When a brand uses "push" marketing, they put their message directly in front of consumers through advertising or other promotions. "Push" marketing is active. Conversely, "pull" marketing is passive, with marketers trying to draw consumers to them organically. As an artist, understanding and implementing both strategies is key.

While there are humans making decisions about Spotify's platform, its AI is paying attention to everything happening on it as well. Knowing this means being able to take advantage of Spotify in ways that help both push and pull tactics. Doing so allows you to implement an integrated plan. Push marketing drives followers to your music and engages Spotify's algorithmic playlisting. This in turn generates pull marketing on your behalf via Spotify's recommendations.

Lots of effort goes into trying to get on third-party and editorial playlists, and both are important for generating attention. However, creating your own inbound traffic is important too. This is the push part of your strategy. Run campaigns that share links customized for individual services and from each of your social platforms. This increases the focus on your music. If you can get enough fans to click through, there will be a spike in traffic when multiple users listen simultaneously. Driving this off-platform traffic to Spotify will be detected, and if you make the spike big enough, the chance your music gets added to an algorithmic playlist increases.

This highlights the importance of release day messaging. Release day is the best moment to focus attention on your music. Sharing a link is one way, and the right call to action will get followers to click through and listen. There are other methods too, including making your own playlist that includes a focus track and then sharing the playlist link, running a pre-save campaign, using the "Artist Pick", and encouraging influencers to point their followers to your music. Be creative here!

These methods all demonstrate push marketing, putting links to your music directly in front of your fans. These are effective tactics, not just on their own, but in how they can get Spotify actively working for you through algorithm playlisting. Driving traffic that triggers Spotify's algorithmic playlists should be half your plan. The other half is making its recommendation engine work for you.

One of the things I tell both clients and students about marketing is that they need to identify their audience. Targeting makes for more efficient marketing, as identifying the people who are interested makes it easier and cheaper to reach them. Spotify does this automatically. Each user has a "Discover Weekly" playlist tailored to their individual listening habits. There are recommendations on user homepages and via the "Fans Also Like" section on artist pages. Introducing new music to users is an important feature; it draws users to the platforms and keeps them engaged. Use this information as part of your own audience targeting. If Spotify identifies your music as similar to another artist, then there is a good chance that that artist's listeners will be interested in your music as well.

Once you can generate the kind of traffic that Spotify notices, your music will begin to appear in algorithmic playlists generated for users who have listened to similar artists. This is Spotify's recommendation AI working and where your pull marketing comes in.

Be ready for these potential fans. Their initial point of contact is through your profile, so make sure it's optimized. Take an inventory: are the photos and bio on Spotify up to date and on-brand? Are you utilizing social badges so followers who hear your music on Spotify for the first time can click through and follow you off-platform? Are you utilizing the "Artist Pick" as a way to get mailing list sign-ups or direct potential fans to other sites you control? Are you displaying tour dates and selling merch?

If your push marketing is working, ensure your pull marketing is too. Provide as many ways for new listeners to engage with you on-platform as possible, and then ensure they are drawn to your own sites. Remember, pull marketing isn't forced. Create the conditions by which your target audience can act once they find you. Having a fully-optimized, up-to-date profile accomplishes this.

It's easy to think of DSPs as a goal, that your marketing ends with them. In actuality, DSPs are also a means to your marketing, enabling you to utilize their individual features as part of your efforts. By fully understanding how a platform works, you can take better advantage of it, turning it into an opportunity. Spotify's AI can be a part of this, a place not just to send existing fans to listen, but one where you can target new fans and get them listening too. Done right, these become intertwined, creating an endless feedback loop in which Spotify's AI becomes a key element in your own marketing.

Find out more about Mark at <u>marktavern.com</u>

Spotify Collaborative Playlists

In the Spotify app on your phone, you can create a collaborative playlist and add users as collaborators. This is safer than sharing a link as anyone who has the link will have access to add/remove songs on your playlist.

1. On your phone or tablet, tap **Your Library**.

2. Go to **Playlists**, and select the one you want to collaborate on (keep in mind you can only do this for playlists you've created)

3. Tap the **Add User** button in the header to make the playlist collaborative

4. Start inviting others to add songs and podcast episodes on social media, messaging apps, or simply by copying and pasting the link

Spotify Deleted Playlists Recovery

If you deleted a playlist in Spotify, you have 90 days to retrieve it! Here's how:

1. Log in to spotify.com/account.

2. Click **Recover Playlists** in the menu on the left.

3. Click **Restore** by the playlist you want to recover.

4. Open Spotify and find the restored playlist at the bottom of your playlist collection.

TIP: SO FAR, RECOVERING A RECENTLY DELETED PLAYLIST MAY ALSO RECOVER ALL FOLLOWERS. THIS IS EXTREMELY VALUABLE FOR ACCIDENTAL DELETIONS AND SAVES YOU STARTING FROM ZERO AGAIN.

Spotify Fans Also Like Section

If you visit an artist profile on Spotify and look at the Fans Also Like tab, you may be wondering how these related artists are being generated. According to Spotify, the Fans Also Like tab on your artist profile is determined by algorithms, using a combination of your fans' listening habits, music discussions and trends happening around the internet.

If you've recently had your music added to Spotify or perhaps you have had to request a separation of your music from an artist with the same name, there is a good chance that your Fans Also Like artists are way off.

For instance, I once worked with a house music producer who shares a name with a children's singer. For obvious reasons, he swiftly wanted to correct his related artists. To correct the related artists, Thomas Garcia signed up for an account with last.fm. The next step was logging into last.fm, going to **Settings**, then **Applications** and opting to connect for Spotify Scrobbling and Spotify Playback.

Last.fm will keep track of your listening history within Spotify and will automatically start to piece together other users listening history. My suggestion is to create a new playlist, say 20 or 30 songs long, including music from both the artist and similar artists you'd like to be related with. Next, share this with some friends or fans and ask them to play it through once or twice (*only* once or twice, no cheating the system unless you want to see your music removed from Spotify). Just make sure your listeners log into their last.fm account and connect to Spotify first.

If all goes well, as it did in my experiment, within a few weeks you should see your related artists start to change and hopefully be more relevant to your music.

Spotify's Personalized Playlists

Contributed by Chris Robley

Don't ignore the power of personalized playlists. It's easy to get distracted by the big official editorial lists that have thousands or millions of followers. It's even easier to get discouraged if you don't end up on one of them!

Spotify's system is constantly working in the background to deliver your music to the right listeners, one listener at a time. That might not feel like a big win or a huge headline, but it does help you make a connection. It helps you make fans, one person at a time.

For my last single, something like 60% of my overall streams were driven by algorithmic activity. For the first 28 days, when Release Radar was delivering the bulk of that interaction, I was getting great engagement ratios too. Not quantity, but quality.

Do I wish I had a huge quantity of streams? Of course. But it's rare to get the former without the latter, and at least the people who DID hear the song were enjoying it. At the end of the day, thanks to Spotify's recommendation engine, that's a kind of success.

Find out more about Chris at <u>chrisrobley.com</u>

Spotify Playlist Cleanup

Take a look at your playlists. There's a good chance some are in need of a little TLC. Here are some tools I use to make sure my playlists are always in good order:

Removing Duplicate Songs

Spotify Dedup is a nifty website that removes duplicated songs from your playlists and saved songs. It can be found at https://jmperezperez.com/spotify-dedup/

Removing Unavailable Tracks

Some songs have since been removed from Spotify or are only available in certain countries. To some users, they will appear grayed out and are unplayable. Here's how to find and remove them:

On the desktop app, go into **Settings** and select **Show Unavailable Songs in Playlists**.

Any Spotify user can turn this option on and see songs in playlist that either are not available in their territory or have since been removed from Spotify (but not yet removed from the playlist). It's a good opportunity to clean up your playlist.

Spotify Genre List

Every Noise at Once (Everynoise.com) is a deep dive into music genres, songs by city and so much more. I use this to discover new genres (Emo Trap or Pirate Metal anyone?).

Here's the explanation directly from their website:

"Every Noise at Once is an ongoing attempt at an algorithmically-generated, readability-adjusted scatter-plot of the musical genre-space, based on data tracked and analyzed for 5,521 genres by Spotify".

Yep, you read correctly... 5,521 genres at time of writing!

Everynoise was created by Glenn McDonald. Glenn is Spotify's genre taxonomist and shares some mind-blowing data through this website and @EveryNoise on Twitter.

Spotify Search Shortcuts

    Spotify search is commonly used for finding songs, artists and playlists but there is so much more you can do. These search keywords are particularly useful when finding music from a specific record label, genre, release in a specific year or range of years.

    All of the keywords below are to be entered into the Spotify search bar. Type in the text below to try this out yourself.

Search by Record Label Name

label: (record label name)

label:universal

If the label is multiple words add a + between each word

label:tommy+boy

Search by Genre

genre: (genre name)

genre:rap

Search by Year

year: (year or year range)

year:2012 or *year:2012-2018*

You can use this to create a Best of 1990s playlist or even a playlist dedicated to your favorite record label and/or genre. By using these keywords, you will be able to discover or rediscover many songs for your playlists.

In the search results, you can then sort by artist name or song title. This will help with the sorting process as you will see multiple releases featuring the same song. You don't want to add multiple versions of the same song into your playlist.

TIP: IT'S MUCH EASIER TO CLICK AND DRAG THESE INTO YOUR PLAYLIST AS YOU DISCOVER THEM. ALTERNATIVELY YOU CAN RIGHT CLICK ON THE SONG AND THEN CHOOSE THE PLAYLIST YOU WOULD LIKE TO ADD IT TO.

Spotify Listener Apps

There's lots of quirky, fun and useful apps that have been created for Spotify listeners. Here's a few worth checking out.

Stations by Spotify
stations.spotify.com

An endless radio stream powered by Spotify.

Spotify for Pets
pets.byspotify.com

Get your Pet Playlist. Music for our best friends.

Soundtrack Your Workout
soundtrackyourworkout.byspotify.com

Uses your listening habits and inputs to create the perfect mix.

Soundtrack Your Ride
soundtrackyourride.byspotify.com

Sync up, customize and get the perfect playlist for your ride.

Spotify Duo: The Ultimate Love Experience
duolovesongs.byspotify.com

Create a personalized love playlist for your relationship.

Spotify Kids
explorethekidsapp.byspotify.com

Sample songs from the Kids app via your favorite emojis.

RapCaviar Day 1 Club
day1club.byspotify.com

Prove which rappers you've been listening to the longest on Spotify.

Spotify HIIT
pumped.byspotify.com

Create a personalized HIIT workout and exercise with music you love. Try Spotify Pumped for free to pump up your fitness.

Spotify Fan Study
fanstudy.byspotify.com

A super detailed study into fan behavior and how it translates into Spotify. The first study showed how many fans come to Spotify from links shared on LinkedIn, Discord and other platforms.

Musixmatch

Musixmatch is not a music streaming platform per se, but they do deliver lyrics to multiple platforms. They even translate lyrics into other languages and can synchronize them in time with the music. I've mentioned them previously, so if you haven't signed up, now is the time.

Anyone can contribute lyrics which are then verified and made available in a number of apps. These include Spotify, Apple Music, Amazon Music, Shazam, Instagram and even Google search results. Artists can also get verified accounts by signing up at musixmatch.com.

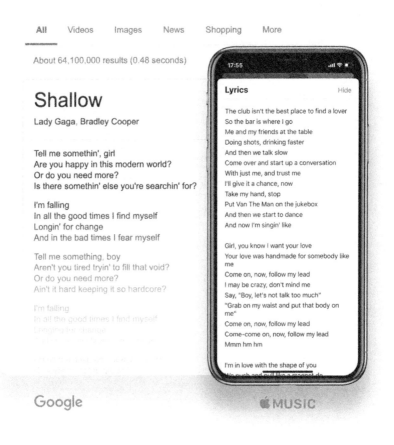

Deezer Backstage

Deezer is available in over 180 countries and is one of the first major DSPs in many of these countries. This means that in many of these countries, such as France, there are more Deezer subscribers than Spotify or Apple Music.

Deezer Backstage launched mid 2020 and is available to artists, managers and labels at backstage.deezer.com

If your request doesn't get a response after a few weeks you can politely escalate with @DeezerHelp on Twitter. I waited three weeks before tweeting and asking them to review my request. Please note that they will ask for the artist name, who requested access (artist, manager or label) and the email address entered on the form. I did this and within 2 days I had access for multiple artists.

Deezer Artist Profile Highlight

Deezer allows you to highlight a track, album or playlist on your artist page. This is similar to the "Artists Pick" option in Spotify.

Go to the Artist Edition page in Deezer Backstage. Under the highlight section, use the Search function to find the content (track, album or playlist) you want to highlight.

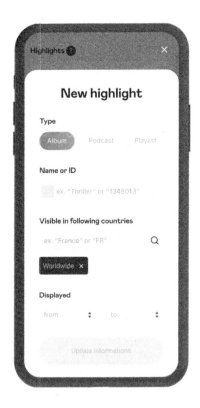

TIP: FOR EASIER SEARCHING, USE THE ID AT THE END OF THE DEEZER URL. (E.G. IF THE DEEZER URL FOR A TRACK IS HTTPS://WWW.DEEZER.COM/TRACK/ 1143579692) COPY THE NUMBERS ONLY. 1143579692 IS THE DEEZER TRACK ID. YOU CAN PASTE THAT INTO THE SEARCH BOX TO FIND THE EXACT RESULT.

Select the country where you want the highlighted content to be visible. To display it to your entire fanbase, select **Worldwide**.

Choose how long you want the content to be highlighted on your page.

Highlight

Pocket Songs
by Dua Lipa

6,538 fans

.

Deezer Artist Playlists

You can feature up to two playlists on your Deezer Artist Profile.

To do this, you will first need to create two playlists as a user in Deezer (logged in to the app as a listener). You can update these playlists with new music anytime. Once you have created your playlists follow these steps:

- Email support@deezer.com with the subject "Artist Profile Update: Artist Name."

- Include two links to playlists you have created. These will be added to your artist profile as artist playlists.

- Deezer also requires the URL of your artist profile and your Deezer username in the email.

Deezer Web Widget

Deezer's embeddable web widget is available worldwide,. Even if Deezer isn't available in your country, you can still create a widget.

You can embed an album, playlist, track, artist, podcast, or podcast episode. The widget can be included on artist websites, articles, blogs and posts. You can create a widget at widget.deezer.com, or if you use Deezer on the web, click the **Share** menu.

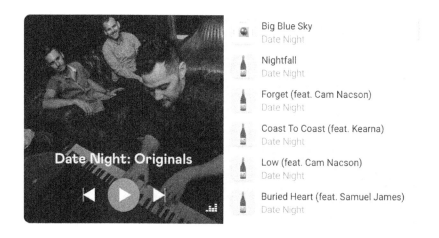

TIP: CREATE A DEDICATED LANDING PAGE FOR EACH STREAMING PLATFORM ON YOUR WEBSITE. THIS WILL ALLOW YOU TO INCLUDE DIRECT LINKS TO YOUR MUSIC AND PLAYLISTS ON THAT SPECIFIC DSP.

Amazon Music for Artists

Amazon Music is fast becoming a major player in the music streaming world. Artists can get access to their profiles, some helpful tools for selling merch and even integrations with Twitch. Amazon Music for Artists launched in 2020 and is available on the web at artists.amazon.com and as a mobile app for iOS and Android devices.

You will need an Amazon account to be able to sign in and claim your profile. Creating an Amazon account is free and can be used to log in to multiple Amazon products including Twitch.

Once logged in, you can request access on the main screen. You will be greeted with a form where you should add as much information as you can to prove that you are the artist or should have access to that artist (e.g. you are a manager, label or distributor for the artist).

To get expedited access, you can log in with your distributor credentials if you distribute your music to Amazon Music using CD Baby, DistroKid or TuneCore. This is the quickest known way to get access and skip any waiting periods while someone at Amazon verifies your request.

Amazon Music Artist Profile

You can upload a profile photo and cover photo in Amazon Music for Artists. This can be done by going to the Profile and Tools screen at artists.amazon.com or clicking the person icon in the app on your phone.

These images will need to meet certain guidelines, which you can see in the app, to make sure that your images will be accepted.

There is currently no known way to add a biography to an artist profile on Amazon Music.

Amazon Music and Twitch Linking

You can link your Twitch account to your Amazon Music artist profile. This allows users of Amazon Music to view your Twitch livestreams directly in the Twitch or Amazon Music App (on your artist profile). It also notifies all your followers when you go live.

To set this up, log in to the Amazon Music for Artists app and click the profile icon (bottom right corner in the mobile app) or click **Profile and Tools** on the Amazon Music for artists website. From here, you can connect your Twitch channel.

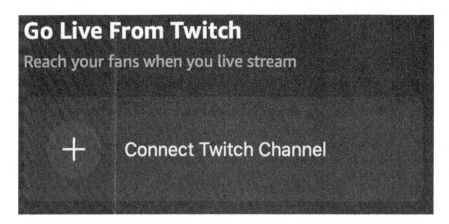

Artists can also work their way up to become Twitch affiliates, which allows fans to subscribe to their channel and send tips known as "Bits".

Twitch Prime users get a monthly subscription included and they can use that to subscribe to any Twitch channel and support the artist directly.

Amazon Music Merch

Artists can now create their own merchandise page on Amazon and link it to their Amazon Music artist page. Check out these examples from Taylor Swift, Mary J. Blige and AC/DC.

amazon.com/acdc

amazon.com/maryjblige

amazon.com/taylorswift

All the latest information, request forms and integrations can be found at artists.amazonmusic.com/merch.

Amazon Music Editorial Playlist Pitching

Amazon Music recommends asking your record label, distributor or manager to pitch music to their editorial team for playlist and station programming consideration. However, as listed on the FAQ on their website, if you are an independent artist with no label or manager you can send your music to music-pitches@amazon.com.

Don't have a subscription to Amazon Music? You can go to music.amazon.com in most web browsers (screenshot from Google Chrome below), without the need to sign in. You can search the music library and copy share links to tracks, albums, artists, podcasts and music videos.

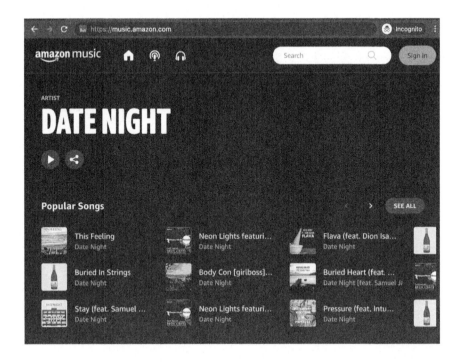

Amazon Music Social Media Tags

Tag the relevant Amazon accounts in each post on social media. Amazon Music is one of the newer DSPs, so they tend to be more responsive on social media. Tag these accounts in your posts and they may respond.

Facebook: AmazonMusic (Global) and AmazonMusicDeSchlager (Germany)

Twitter: @AmazonMusic, @AmazonMusicUK, @AmazonMusicJP, @AmazonMusicMX, @AmazonMusicIN

Instagram: @AmazonMusic, @AmazonMusicUK, @AmazonMusicDE, @AmazonMusicJP, @AmazonMusicMX, @AmazonMusicBR, @AmazonPrimeMusicIN

Amazon Music has also started creating social media accounts for specific genres. If you create Hip-Hop, R&B or German Deutchrap you should also tag these handles in your posts.

Genre Handles: @rotation (Hip-Hop and R&B) and @auf_level (German Deutchrap)

Amazon Music suggests tagging @AmazonMusic over using #AmazonMusic - this is clearly mentioned in their online documentation. They also say that by tagging them in your posts it "makes it easy for us to find, engage, and share your posts to our followers".

Amazon Music Using Alexa

Have your followers request you directly from their Alexa device. The Amazon Music team pays close attention to the number of requests for an artist through Alexa. Requests can be made to Alexa using artist name, album name, song title or by singing part of the song lyrics.

Artists can also see how many people have requested their music by song, album, artist or by singing or speaking part of the lyrics. This can be found in Amazon Music for Artists.

TIP: ADD YOUR SONG LYRICS TO AMAZON THROUGH LYRICFIND OR MUSIXMATCH AS FANS MAY NOT KNOW YOUR SONG TITLE BUT CAN SPEAK (OR SING) THE LYRICS TO ALEXA.

Get your fans to follow you on their Alexa device to receive notifications when you release new music. Fans can simply say "Alexa, follow ARTIST NAME on Amazon Music". If you have an artist name that is unique to pronounce you can teach your fans how to pronounce the name correctly in video posts on social media. You can also speak directly with your label or distributor and inform them of the correct pronunciation of your artist name, and they can deliver that information to Amazon for you.

TIP: WITH MULTIPLE DSPS SUPPORTING VOICE, YOU CAN ALSO MAKE REQUESTS VIA ALEXA TO FOLLOW OTHER SERVICES (E.G. "ALEXA FOLLOW ARTIST NAME ON SPOTIFY"). AS LONG AS YOU HAVE LINKED THAT DSP ON YOUR ALEXA-ENABLED DEVICE, YOU CAN MAKE THIS REQUEST.

Anghami for Artists

Anghami launched in 2012 as the first legal music streaming platform and digital distribution company in the Middle East. Anghami allows the uploading of songs, albums, podcasts, and music videos directly to its platform, bypassing a distributor.

It's worth mentioning that Anghami is available in a number of countries worldwide but does not currently have agreements for all content to be available in all countries. In other words, most music is available on Anghami for listeners in the Middle East but may not show on Anghami in the US.

One way to see if your music is on Anghami is to open an incognito web browser window and search for **Artist Name - Song Anghami**. Your song may show up in the search results, and you can grab the URL for the artist, song or album.

Anghami Artist Profile

Once you have access and are signed into your Dashboard account, click on **My Artist Profile**.

On this page you can do the following:

- Upload an artist profile image or choose to use the picture from their Facebook page

- Update the artist name in English and Arabic

- Edit the music language (Arabic or International)

- Add a biography in English and/or Arabic

- Add links to Facebook and Twitter

Click **Update Profile** when done. These changes are not instant. Anghami staff will review them and send an email with approval or rejection usually within a few days.

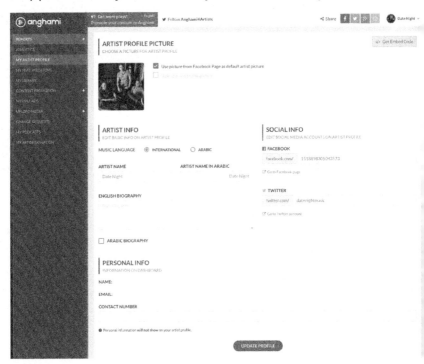

Anghami Direct Music Uploads

As mentioned, Anghami has a rare offering which allows artists to upload music directly. This means you can bypass a distributor. If you previously distributed music to Anghami, you can simply uncheck Anghami as a store for future music releases with your distributor. Your distributor will then continue to handle all other stores while you are responsible for uploading your music to Anghami.

Uploading your music yourself to Anghami allows detailed revenue-based data with financial reports, streams by song and streams by country.

The upload form is relatively straight forward. Even better, you can also upload songs, albums, podcasts, DJ mixes and compilations through this form.

You can also upload videos, using either a video file from your computer or a YouTube link. These will be connected to an existing song you have previously uploaded to allow fans to opt for watching the music video and accompany visuals as an alternative to streaming just the audio.

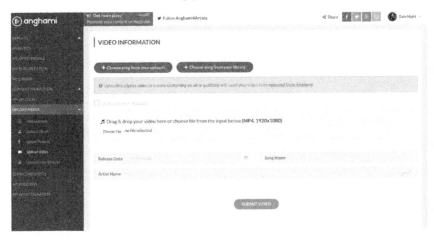

Anghami Editorial Playlist Pitching

The Anghami for Artists mobile app now shows an exciting option that is coming soon for direct playlist pitching. While there is no more detail yet, it's a great reason for artists to sign up and claim access now so they can be first in line as soon as this feature becomes available. Keep in mind that when Spotify first launched their editorial playlist submission tool, roughly one in every seven tracks was being added to an editorial playlist as a result. It's definitely worth signing up and being one of the first when this is available

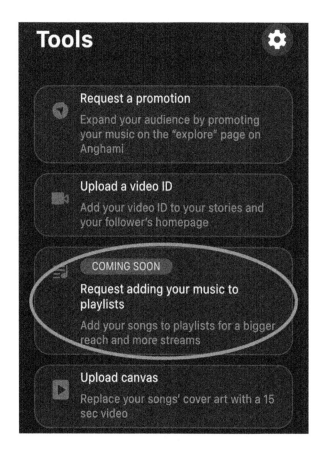

Qobuz

Qobuz is geared towards audiophiles, largely due to their integration with high-end home audio equipment. Their curation is completely human and it shows. The playlists are shorter, heavily curated and they are not afraid to showcase music from less established artists.

Artist bios are delivered to Qobuz from TiVo (yep, the same company that has pioneered the magic TV recording box). TiVo's database is also shared at Allmusic.com for biographical information. To include your bio on Qobuz, send an email to TiVo at content.music@tivo.com. Be warned, it can take a few weeks for this data to appear on Allmusic.com and then on Qobuz.

Album reviews are written in-house by the Qobuz team. There is no official process for submitting music for consideration for review at this time.

You can change your artist photo by reaching out through the customer service portal https://www.qobuz.com/us-en/help/contact with a link to your artist page.

Genius

    Genius is a community of music lovers and artists sharing their knowledge and stories behind the music. Genius also delivers lyrics and extra information to various streaming services. You can get verified at genius.com.

    Once verified, you will be able to share accurate lyrics, hidden meanings/stories behind songs/song lyrics and even reach out to fans that are already annotating your music on the site.

Napster

Napster only allows you to upload one image at this time. To do this, fill out the form at https://help.napster.com/hc/en-us/requests/new. Be sure to include the URL to your Artist page so they know where to upload it. The dimensions for the image have to be 1500 x 1000 and a JPEG file. The live chat on Napster's website is also quite helpful: https://help.napster.com/hc/articles/218661367.

Tidal

Tidal doesn't currently provide any artist tools or apps. That being said, social media links, bios and photos can be added to an artist profile by sending an email.

In fact, by going to Jay-Z's artist profile you can see an example of how much additional information can be added. There are links to his social media, an updated bio and photos.

https://listen.tidal.com/artist/7804

Send an email to artistsupport@tidal.com with two photos, links to your social media, a short biography and the URL to your artist profile on Tidal (e.g. tidal.com/artist/5124128).

Tidal is similar to other DSPs in that you can view an artist page without having an account or being logged in. In the screenshots below, I went to listen.tidal.com and searched for the Date Night artist page in Google Chrome. https://listen.tidal.com/artist/5124128

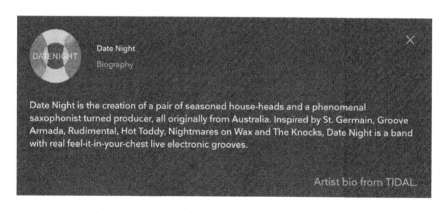

Apple Music

Apple Music launched in 2015 and is available in over 100 countries worldwide. If you don't have an Apple device or Apple ID, you can still see what is offered on Apple Music by going to music.apple.com from your computer. Prior to 2020, users could do this by navigating to beta.music.apple.com, which is still functional as well.

You can even browse through the music selection on Apple Music without signing in. This allows you to make sure your music is available and see what your artist profile looks like without having to pay for a subscription. You can also see if your song has been featured on a playlist, chart, or on one of the homepage screens. Of course, you still need a subscription to fully stream any music.

You can also easily change the country to see the homepage in various countries as programming varies by country. This is available at the bottom of the screen.

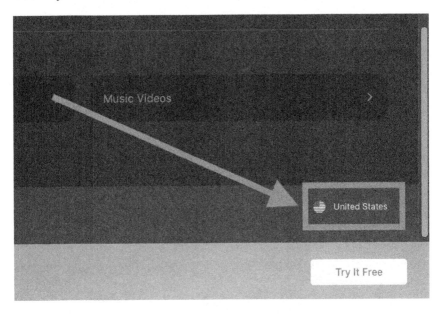

Apple Music for Artists

Artists, labels and managers can sign up to Apple Music for Artists at artists.apple.com and request access to one or multiple artists.

Alternatively, access can also be requested in the Apple Music for Artists app, currently available only on Apple iOS devices.

Requests can be fast-tracked for independent artists through their distributor. Currently, the following distributors have a way to expedite access to Apple Music for Artists:

- CD Baby

- DistroKid

- ONErpm

- TuneCore

- UnitedMasters

Apple Music also includes Shazam insights. Fun fact: Any time someone with an Apple devices says "Hey Siri, what song is this?", the answer is delivered from Shazam and counts as a Shazam, even if you don't have the Shazam app installed.

Apple Music Artist Data

Once you have access, let's walk through the features in Apple Music for Artists.

Overview

The Overview panel is a quick summary of plays, average daily listeners, iTunes song purchases and Shazams.

You can choose to see stats going as far back as the lifetime of the artist on the platform or as recent as the past week.

Insights

The Insights section provides a quick glance at specific milestones, letting you know where your music is taking off around the world. This tells you about editorial playlist adds, Shazam milestones and stream milestones.

Insights

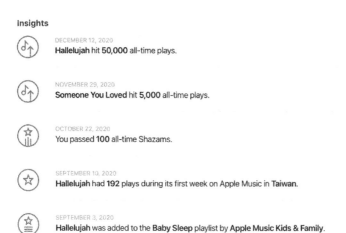

DECEMBER 12, 2020
Hallelujah hit **50,000** all-time plays.

NOVEMBER 29, 2020
Someone You Loved hit **5,000** all-time plays.

OCTOBER 22, 2020
You passed **100** all-time Shazams.

SEPTEMBER 10, 2020
Hallelujah had **192** plays during its first week on Apple Music in **Taiwan**.

SEPTEMBER 3, 2020
Hallelujah was added to the **Baby Sleep** playlist by **Apple Music Kids & Family**.

Trends

The Trends section allows you to customize a graph to give a visual representation of the numbers for your artist. You can use the drop-down menus to filter your stream counts by individual songs, playlists, locations, ages, genders and more.

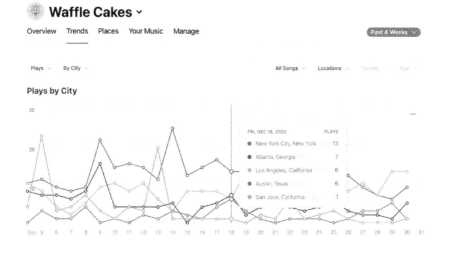

Places

The data in this section allows you to dive deeper into how many plays, listeners and Shazams your music is getting in specific countries or regions.

This can be extremely valuable for routing a tour or targeting social media ads towards fans in a specific city.

Your Music

The Your Music tab shows a summary of plays, average daily listeners, Shazams, radio spins and iTunes purchases.

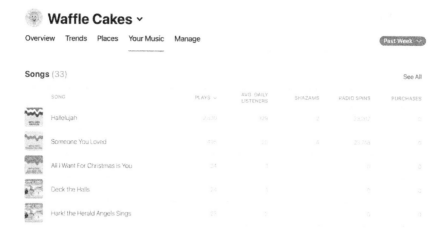

Waffle Cakes ⌄

Overview Trends Places Your Music Manage

Past Week ⌄

Songs (33)   See All

SONG	PLAYS ⌄	AVG. DAILY LISTENERS	SHAZAMS	RADIO SPINS	PURCHASES
Hallelujah					
Someone You Loved					
All I Want For Christmas Is You					
Deck the Halls					
Hark! the Herald Angels Sings					

If you have been added to a playlist, you can also see the number of songs added to that playlist and the number of plays received through that playlist.

Playlists (2)   See All

PLAYLIST	SONGS	PLAYS ⌄
Baby Sleep Apple Music Kids & Family		
Piano Christmas Waffle Cakes		

Downloading Your Data

Apple Music for Artists allows you to download some of this data in CSV (comma separated values) format. This allows you to open the file in your preferred spreadsheet program (Microsoft Excel, Apple Numbers, Google Sheets).

To download data, click the text **See All**.

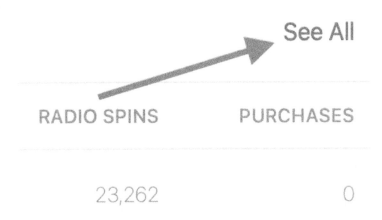

On the next screen, click the square icon with the down arrow. This will automatically launch the download of the CSV file for you.

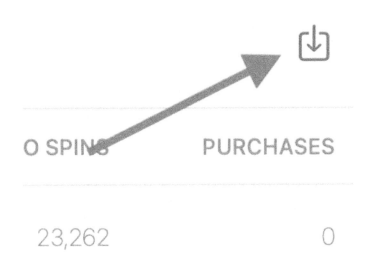

Updating Your Artist Profile Picture

You can change your artist profile picture by clicking the Manage tab, then clicking Upload Image.

Apple is very particular about the artist images. The artist's face must be visible and you can't upload text or a logo used for the artwork. In this example, the artist is an animated drawing, but their face is still clearly viewable so the art was accepted.

Apple Music Marketing Tools

If you are looking for unique ways to share links to music, such as a scannable QR code or embeddable music player, check out this suite of marketing tools from Apple Music. If you happen to also be an affiliate with Apple, you can include your affiliate code when sharing links to Apple Music as well and make a little extra money from sharing music. Pretty cool, huh?

The following tools we're about to cover can all be created at: https://tools.applemediaservices.com/apple-music

Apple Music QR Codes

QR codes are an interactive and effective way to drive more people to a specific website, product, or - in this case - music! Print these on clothing, bumper stickers or even project them onto screens.

Try this out. If you have a newer phone, open the camera and point it at the QR code below.

If all goes well, if you will see the option to open the song in Apple Music.

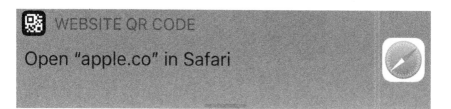

Apple Music Twitter Audio Card

Twitter Audio Cards are a 30-second preview of a song that can be shared within a tweet. They use the album cover art and allow anyone to listen to a 30 second clip of the song without leaving Twitter. Apple Music subscribers can also click the link to hear the song in full. Another nice bonus here is that Apple affiliates can include an affiliate code when generating these previews and can make some money from any subscriptions that occur.

Big Blue Sky
Date Night & Chris Robley - Big Blue Sky on Appl...
tools.applemediaservices.com

Apple Music Artist Playlists

Creating playlists as an artist on Apple Music takes a few steps, but it's well worth the extra steps to give you an edge over the competition.

You will need admin access to the artist in Apple Music for Artists, an Apple Music subscription and the Apple Music app installed on your phone. At time of writing, you can only do via the mobile app.

- Tap the **Library** icon, tap edit, check **Admin**, tap done.

- Tap **Admin**, tap the artist name, tap **New Playlist**.

While the playlists will not currently show in search results or on artist profiles, the links can be shared on social media. Your fans can then save your playlists to their own library, and the playlist curator name will link listeners directly to your artist profile.

*A video walkthrough of this can be found at WorkHardPlaylistHard.com

Apple Music Lyrics

Add lyrics to your music to allow fans to find your song by search or by speaking part of the lyrics. This is also helpful for potential new fans who may only remember part of the lyrics to one of your songs.

Some distributors will offer a way to push lyrics to Apple Music and other streaming platforms. Alternatively, you can send the lyrics directly to the Apple Music team via their contact form (https://artists.apple.com/contact-us). There should be an option for **Submit Your Lyrics**.

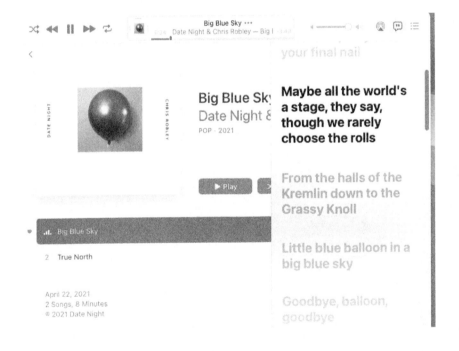

Beatport Artist and Label Profiles

Beatport started as an online music store to purchase extended mixes of music for DJs. In 2019, Beatport Link launched and allowed DJs to stream any song from Beatport to connected DJ equipment.

Beatport allows artists to upload a professional headshot to their artist profile. The artwork must be at least 590 x 404 pixels and a JPEG image. You can do this by going to https://www.jotform.us/form/13105057250

If you are a DJ in addition to a being a producer, you can create your own charts on Beatport at beatport.com/dj/charts/new. You can then add these charts to your artist profile.

If you are a label owner, you can also have your label profile updated as well. Your image must be 500 × 500 pixels, and you can include a bio as well. The label update form and be found at: https://www.jotform.com/form/20221418251.

TIP: MOST INDEPENDENT MUSIC DISTRIBUTORS HAVE THE ABILITY TO DISTRIBUTE MUSIC TO BEATPORT BUT MAY ONLY DO SO UPON REQUEST. THIS IS BECAUSE NOT EVERY GENRE OF MUSIC IS ACCEPTED OR AVAILABLE ON THE PLATFORM. IF YOU MAKE SOME FORM OF ELECTRONIC MUSIC OR HIP-HOP, YOU SHOULD DEFINITELY REACH OUT TO YOUR DISTRIBUTOR TO SEE IF THEY CAN ALSO ADD YOUR MUSIC TO BEATPORT.

Beatport Hype

Running your own label? Beatport Hype is an official Beatport promotional platform, with a suite of features to get your music in front of more listeners. It is, however, only available to selected label partners. The monthly cost is less than a Netflix subscription, and Beatport claims that "on average, labels signed up to Beatport Hype have seen an increase of more than 70% in track sales".

This is owned and operated by Beatport themselves. With 35 million unique visitors a year and 25,000 tracks added every week, it's a great opportunity to invest in some extra promotion to get your music heard.

https://hype.beatport.com

Submitting your music through this platform also allows your music to be eligible for dedicated Hype charts including the Hype Top 10, which features on the Beatport homepage.

Pandora Artist Marketing Platform

Pandora is a music streaming platform with close to 60 million monthly listeners in the United States. Artists from anywhere in the world can get access to some awesome tools to reach and grow their audience on Pandora.

Currently, Pandora is only available to listeners in America, but there's nothing stopping artists from all over the world from having a presence on the platform.

Pandora provides a number of extremely useful tools for artists to promote their music and connect with their fans. These are all available through their Artist Marketing Platform (AMP) located at amp.pandora.com

If you are unable to claim your AMP account, you can send an email to Pandora's support team at amp-support@pandora.com.

Pandora Submission Tool

Distributing your music to Pandora is only half of the work. Pandora is a human-curated collection of music. To make your music available on all of Pandora's services, you need to fill out a brief form.

Pandora does have an independent artist submission tool that allows your music to be reviewed and considered by Pandora for programming inclusion on their radio stations. To use this, you will first need that AMP account.

Independent artists can use a distributor such as CD Baby or DistroKid to get their music on Pandora. Once music has been distributed, artists can submit their music at amp.pandora.com/submit.

You can find a release to submit using its UPC or searching by song name. If you are submitting an album, choose one favorite track to put forward for consideration. You will then select a genre and write a description of 4,000 characters or less. There is currently no option to tag moods or keywords in the song submission.

Once a submission is approved, it will be analyzed in the Music Genome Project® and made available on all Pandora platforms.

Pandora Featured Tracks

Pandora allows you to feature up to six tracks per year. Featured tracks will gain an increase in spins across Pandora radio stations in an effort to gain audience feedback. Listeners can vote with a thumbs up or down when they listen to your featured track.

As a bonus, you can do this for any track that was released within the last 12 months. The song will need to have at least 10 spins in the last 7 days to be eligible. (Pro tip: Those 10 spins can come from the same person. Just between us, of course.)

The feature selection form is very short, and there is no review process. The song will simply be featured on the date range you specify. One clever use I've seen of this feature is selecting a holiday song that came out 11 months ago to feature as the lead up to the holiday season in the current year. This way, you can potentially give a song another chance at being heard, especially if it revolves around a specific time of the year like a holiday.

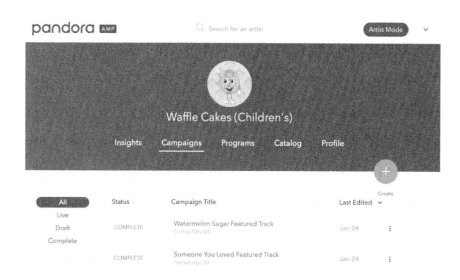

Pandora Stories

Pandora "Stories" are artist-curated playlists and mixtapes (aka "Stations") comprised of music and comedy tracks from Pandora's library. Anyone can create these, not just artists. You can even record your own voice tracks that can be attached to specific songs or set to play between tracks in sequential order.

This is a great opportunity to share some behind-the-scenes stories, fan messages or promotional reminders about your music.

You can request for access to create Stories at: https://www.ampplaybook.com/pandora-stories-signup.

Pandora Artist Audio Messages

Artist Audio Messages (AAMs) are short, 15-second audio notes to your fans. They can be used to promote releases, tour dates, say thank you or intro/outro a song.

These messages also show a photo and a CTA (call to action). This can be a "tap here to buy tickets" in the text or a "tap the link on your screen to listen now" inserted in the audio.

AAMs can run for up to one year once live. You can also set these messages to only play to listeners in specific locations. This is particularly useful if you're promoting a tour where you may only be performing in 5 cities. You can target listeners in those cities with your message.

AMPcast allows you to record and upload messages from your phone within the Pandora App. You will need to log in with the same credentials you use for Pandora AMP.

Pandora Artist Bios

Pandora does not have a way for artists to directly update their biography at this time. Artist bios are hosted by TiVo (yep, still the same company I mentioned in the Qobuz section). TiVo's database is also shared at Allmusic.com.

To include your bio on Pandora, you will need to send an email to TiVo at content.music@tivo.com. It can take a few weeks for this data to appear on Allmusic.com and then on Pandora.

Pandora Fresh Cuts Station

The team at Pandora curates a station that is focused on breaking artists that engage with their artist marketing platform (AMP) and their account on social media. This <u>Fresh Cuts station</u> is currently open for submissions by posting a link to your track on Twitter and tagging @pandoraAMP in the post. Be sure to include the link to your track on Pandora and not another streaming platform. You'd be surprised how many times I've seen artists do this!

Pandora Lyrics

Pandora's lyrical content is hosted by LyricFind. To add lyrics and have them displayed on Pandora, you'll need to contact LyricFind through their website or via their distributor.

Looking for another reason to add your lyrics? Some people don't know the name of a song but they can recall and type part of the lyrics. They can speak or sing them to their smart speaker device. Alexa, Google and Siri can all sync with Pandora. By adding lyrics, you allow people to find your song through key words.

Pandora Track Reporting

Pandora provides comprehensive insights into a track's performance including streams, radio spins, interactive plays, station adds and thumbs up.

All of this artist data can be exported as a CSV, allowing you to import it into the spreadsheet program of your choice. There are dedicated reporting pages for each track with line graphs for daily tends and a "source breakdown", which shows what programs a track is being streamed on.

TikTok for Artists

TikTok is one of the most addictive social media platforms of our time. Artists have opportunities to grow their audience on here through one of two ways.

1. Users create videos using your music.

2. You create your own videos and grow a following on your TikTok profile.

Here's what to do when you first download the app:

– Pick a username consistent with your other platforms. Then connect your YouTube and Instagram profiles for cross-platform growth (e.g. @askmikewarner is my handle on social media, including TikTok).

– Warm up your account for a few days before you start posting. Use the app like a regular user, follow profiles and leave thoughtful comments on content you like. This is important to do before posting your first video because it teaches TikTok about your account.

– Post one high quality and engaging video with your target audience in mind. You can look at some of the first TikTok videos posted by artists similar to you for inspiration. With your first few posts, TikTok's algorithm will be working to understand who you are, what you are about and who to show your TikTok videos to.

– Make sure to post consistently but not too much. As a guide, in the first two weeks, post two videos a week at different times and watch to see which video has more engagement. Pay attention to things like time of day posted, hashtags used, content, quality, length.

You can link to a web version of your public TikTok profile to share anywhere. Simply use this URL format: If your TikTok handle is @askmikewarner, your TikTok web link is tiktok.com/@askmikewarner.

Most content on the platform can be viewed on the web browser without even being logged in.

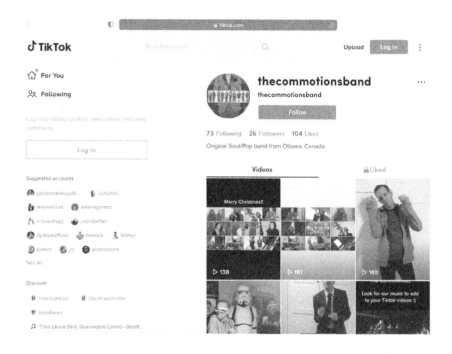

TIP: IF YOU FIND TIKTOK USERS CREATING VIDEOS WITH YOUR MUSIC, YOU CAN SAVE OR SHARE THESE VIDEOS TO SOCIAL MEDIA. IT'S FREE CONTENT AND A GREAT WAY TO THANK THE CREATOR.

TikTok Audio Preview Start Times

Ever find yourself scrolling through TikTok and notice that the catchiest part of the song is always used? This is no coincidence. When music is uploaded through a distributor, there is an option to specify the start time for audio previews. This means that if people preview the song in iTunes or Apple Music, it will begin playing exactly at the timestamp you specified the preview to start. This also applies to TikTok and is super valuable if someone wants to include your song in their video.

It's no secret that hit songs like Lizzo - Truth Hurts have a very strategic preview start time. For those that aren't familiar, the clip starts with "I just took a DNA test, turns out, I'm 100% _____."

Preview clip start time
TikTok, Apple Music, iTunes

○ Let streaming services decide
● Let me specify when the good part starts

Many distributors will allow artists to go and update the preview clip start time for music that has already been released. This avoids the need to redistribute music that is already live.

TIP: SOME ARTISTS HAVE SEEN SIGNIFICANT SUCCESS WITH A SONG ON TIKTOK. WHEN A CLIP GOES VIRAL, USERS START SEARCHING FOR THE SONG IT USES. MAKE SURE YOU HAVE ADDED YOUR LYRICS IN THE SERVICES MENTIONED EARLIER. SOME ARTISTS HAVE EVEN RENAMED A TRACK SO THE SONG TITLE MATCHES THE MOST RECOGNIZABLE PART OF THE LYRICS.

YouTube Official Artist Channels

As an artist, there's a good chance some of your music is already on YouTube in one form or another. You may have uploaded some live footage, or your distributor may have added it to one of those "your band name - topic" channels. Now there's a way to merge all of these videos from various channels into one official artist channel.

Now, before you say "I looked into this previously and it was too hard because I didn't have _____" - Just stop right there. Things have changed.

Previously you needed three music videos to be delivered to YouTube via a distributor before you could claim your official artist channel, but now the requirement is three *releases* delivered via a distributor. This means even audio releases count!

According to artists.youtube.com, all artists can now claim an OAC (Official Artist Channel). YouTube launched OACs in 2018, allowing artists to merge multiple YouTube channels into one official channel. If you have songs uploaded by a record label on one channel or songs uploaded by VEVO or your distributor (also know as Topic channels), these will now be merged into one official artist channel.

Official Artist Channels can be spotted because there will be a musical note after the artists name as pictured below.

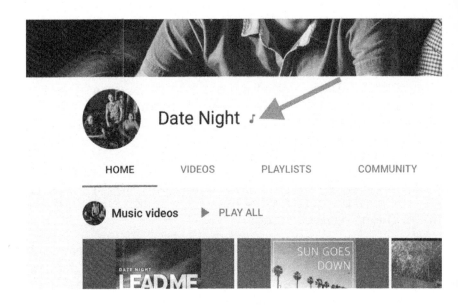

OACs will have a playlist called **Music Videos** that features all songs that have been distributed to YouTube. These no longer appear under **Artist Name (Topic)** channels and will automatically be added to this playlist on the Official Artist Channel on YouTube.

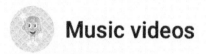 **Music videos** ▶ PLAY ALL

Watermelon Sugar   Hark! th

Waffle Cakes ♪   Waffle C:

39 views • 2 months ago   1 view •

Here's what you need to know about YouTube OACs

Organized content: The channel layout automatically organizes your discography into an album section and your official music videos into new playlists. To ensure a consistent fan experience across YouTube, you can't edit these playlists. However, you can place a separate section above your locked video and album sections to promote anything you like.

Discoverability in search: When your fans search for you on YouTube, they'll be linked directly to your OAC from your watch card on the right side of the screen.

Promotional content: Choose what you want to highlight in the dedicated promotional shelf and in the featured video slot.

Fan engagement: One verified, unified channel where you can directly reach and engage with your fans on YouTube.

These above notes were taken from this support article on YouTube's support page:

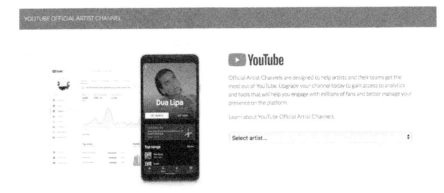

The latest YouTube artist support article states: "If you work with a label, digital distributor, or have a partner manager, get in touch with them to get an Official Artist Channel." However, no form or link is provided, and there is no mention of which digital distributors are able to handle Official Artist Channel requests.

So artists that are signed to a record label or have a partner manager for YouTube are set, but what about the independent artists? I did some research and compiled a list of digital distributors that can help:

CD Baby - Available in the tools section.

DistroKid - In the settings menu, scroll down and click on the YouTube Official Artist Channel link. If you are already signed in to your DistroKid account go directly to distrokid.com/YouTubeOfficialArtistChannels.

Once you have claimed your channel, you will receive a confirmation email from YouTube with new ways you can connect with your fans using Community Posts, Mobile Live, Tickets and Comment Hearts.

YouTube Analytics for Artists

Artists on YouTube are finally getting access to more data and insights! YouTube has finally announced their much-awaited analytics product for artists. Bypassing any beta release, "New YouTube Analytics for Artists" is now live. Yep, the word "new" is part of the title. It's available for all artists with an OAC.

Here's the announcement from studio.youtube.com:

The new Analytics for Artists is here - giving artists the most comprehensive and complete view of their audience, global reach and performance across YouTube. Visit https://studio.youtube.com to check it out. Analytics for Artists will be available for all Official Artist Channels, and provide access to a unique set of features that will equip artists and their teams with the knowledge they need to make the most informed and strategic release plans. In addition to desktop, artists can now easily access these new insights on the YouTube Studio Mobile app, enabling them to get data and notification updates, in real time, whether they are on the road or in the studio.

Artists with an Official Artist Channel can view their stats at studio.youtube.com or through the YouTube Studio App.

Download the YouTube Studio app for Android from Google Play on devices running Android 4.5 and later

Download the YouTube Studio app for iOS from the App Store on iPhones and iPads running iOS 11 and later.

YouTube Artist Image

Studio.youtube.com allows artists with an OAC to add a bio, photos and create artist playlists on their profile. The photos uploaded can be seen on YouTube search, YouTube Charts, the YouTube Music app, playlists, and banners.

YouTube will ask you to upload the same image twice in different dimensions. One of the images will be used on YouTube, while the other will be used in the YouTube Music app.

1. Go to studio.youtube.com

2. On the left, click **Profile**

3. Enter your name and bio.

4. Pick a high-quality photo.

5. Using the pencil icon, add a square profile photo and a rectangular profile photo.

YouTube Artist Bio

Again, this is done by logging in to studio.youtube.com. Once accepted, your bio can be seen on YouTube search, your channel and the YouTube Music App.

To update your bio, select anywhere in the Biography box, enter your bio, and select **Save Bio**. Be sure to follow these guidelines to make sure it doesn't get taken down by YouTube:

- Keep it under 1500 characters. After 150 characters, YouTube Music truncates it and puts the remaining bio behind a "More" link.

- Make sure the content meets their Community Guidelines.

- Keep your bio up to date. Promoting an upcoming album or new release in your bio may go out-of-date quickly.

YouTube Community Posts and Fan Engagement

YouTube OACs also have access to a new feature. In the **Community** tab, artists can create posts with text, images, GIFs, playlists, videos and polls. You can even tag other channels in your posts by using @ followed by the channel name. These posts can also be scheduled for a later date.

In addition to liking and disliking comments on your videos, you can also "heart" comments. Your fans can see when you heart their comments. This allows for re-engagement as they receive a notification when you do.

This is cool!

 1   REPLY

YouTube Guide for Artists

This guide was contributed by a good friend who wanted to remain anonymous.

Best Practice for YouTube Video Optimization:

Artists have a fundamental misunderstanding of what YouTube's core product is. It's not a video/audio hosting service. It's a content recommendation engine.

The key to YouTube's growth as a platform and its value to artists is its "suggested videos" recommendation algorithm. Artists who are already using the platform to discover music and want to make the most of YouTube's recommendation algorithm and tap into its huge global audience of active users should fully optimize their YouTube content along with their channels. This gives the algorithm the correct information it needs to serve their content to new audiences on YouTube.

YouTube Algorithm (Quickly) Explained:

YouTube's recommendation engine serves content using their north star metric of **Watch Time Per Impression**. This means the longer your video can retain a viewer, impacting watch time, the more likely the YT algorithm will be to recommend your content to new audiences. To YouTube, an engaging 15 minute-long content piece has more long term potential reach then a 3 minute long music video, so your long form video content strategy and YouTube strategy should be one and the same.

After release, 80% of a video's views will come within the first 10 days (unless re-inserted into the recommendation algorithm). Subscribers/previous viewers are served a new video within the first 48 hours and YouTube will continue to surface the video within the Home Page/Browse section for the next 10 days before more long term suggestions take over from the 3-6 week mark onwards (if you've satisfied the algorithm!).

The first 48 hours to 10 days of a video's lifetime are crucial to its longterm viability on YouTube, so it pays to maximize your impact at launch by ensuring your content is properly optimized for YouTube. Optimizing video metadata improves search results and YouTube recommendations over time so views continue to flow in incrementally after release.

Youtube Video Optimizations:

NOTE: These video optimizations are only for OAC uploads and don't apply to YouTube Audio products delivered to YouTube via a distributor.

How To Optimize Your Videos

Track Title:

A YT video title is made up of 2 parts. The Information (artist name, content keywords) and The Hook (what happens, emotion driven, tease of content).

Video titles are one of the most important YouTube indexes for search, so you must always ensure you have your critical keywords included when relevant:

- "Official Music Video" for music videos

- "Live" for live performances

- "Artist/Track" names for covers

- "Acoustic" for acoustic renditions etc

- "Location" if relevant to content piece (e.g. "Live at Wembley Arena")

    — "Year" if a video is current or old enough to be nostalgic.

You'll also want to Keep a consistent structure with titles and punctuation for example: Artist Name - Track Name (<Critical Keyword>).

YouTube Thumbnails:

Thumbnails are the important feature of a YT video as it acts as the front window to any potential viewer who may be deciding whether or not to watch your video. This is also the hardest topic for blanket suggested optimizations, as all suggestions are very case-by-case.

Your safest bet is choosing an engaging/eye catching screen grab from within the video. Usually this involves a well lit close up of the artist's face/with eye contact and a conveyed emotion.

The thumbnail must be engaging and there must be synergy between the title and thumbnail.

Inferno - Tell Me Bout It
(Official Music Video)

7.9K views · 1 year ago · 98%

INFERNO - My Way (Official Music Video)

3.5K views · 1 year ago · 97%

Track Meta Description Structure:

A video's meta description is the keyword-rich text that YouTube indexes for search results. You'll want to include as many relevant text/keywords in there as possible without spamming.

Here's a good video description template example, taken from a well-optimized artist video on YouTube.

— The first line of a video's meta description must directly reflect the title of the video.

— Any added copy for context etc.

— Links to any streaming, social or sales sites.

— Song Lyrics - Song lyrics must go in video description in case listeners are searching for the lyrics lyrics on YouTube without knowing the track name.

— Artist bio - Keyword-rich, artist-specific text at the bottom of meta description

Video Keywords

Take advantage of the 500 characters available when adding tags and keep in mind that SEO keywords for musicians are branded and specific. You're looking to align your video keywords with specific terms that users are already searching for on Google when they search for you. (For Example: " <song name> Lyrics", "<Artist Name> Live", "<Artist Name> Acoustic" etc.). This will require some keyword research on your behalf.

A general Template forYouTube keywords would be as follows: Band Specific, Track Specific, Other Top Performing Tracks From That Artist, Lyrics, Band Member Names, Video Specific (eg. Live/Acoustic/Year of recording etc.)

See below for well optimized Keywords from our example YouTube video here.

Tags

Tags can be useful if content in your video is commonly misspelled. Otherwise, tags play a minimal role in helping viewers find your video. Learn more

Enter a comma after each tag

497/500

Video End-Screens

Video End-Screens: A standardized end-screen template across all videos is a must as it creates extended viewing sessions for listeners who finish your videos. Viewers who complete a video are looking for their next content piece to watch, so you want to make sure you provide that to them with an end-screen.

A good template includes the following 3 elements: A Channel Subscribe Button, Link to Official Music Video YT Playlist and the "Best For Audience" algorithmic suggestion that YouTube pulls from an artist's channel. See below for example.

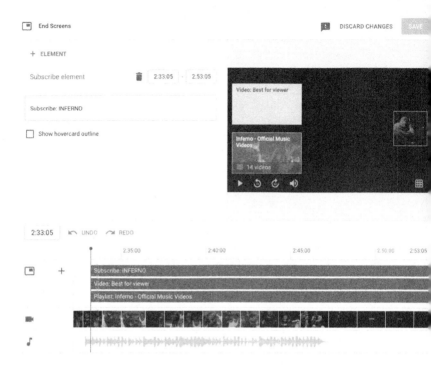

This guide was contributed by a good friend who wanted to remain anonymous.

Bandcamp

Streaming services have forever changed the way fans listen to music, and in the process, as is evidenced by this book, demonstrated a need for artists to rethink how they share, sell and promote their music. For the most part, streaming services do one thing - stream your music. But imagine a platform where a fan can listen to your music and then with one click BUY that music. Not just as an mp3 - It can even be a cd, a vinyl LP, a tape or heck, even a pin, a patch or a t-shirt!

While technically more of a retail platform, the indie artist's beloved Bandcamp functions in some ways very much like a streaming platform. In fact is so much more.

Bandcamp has a detailed site for artists at bandcamp.com/artists

JioSaavn Artist One

JioSaavn (previously known as Saavn and pronounced jee·ow·saa·vn) was founded in 2007. It is the Indian online music streaming service and a digital distributor of Bollywood, English and other regional Indian music across the world.

At time of writing JioSaavn has over 100 million users using the JioSaavn app and website across the world.

JioSaavn has an artist-facing website called Artist One. Register at artists.jiosaavn.com to gain access to data showing where your fans are from.

A cool feature unique to JioSaavn is that it will show you other artists your fans also like and encourage you to collaborate with those artists on a future release to grow your fanbase together.

Artist One was previously known as JioSaavn Artist Insights.

TIP: FOLLOW @JIOSAAVNFORCREATORS ON INSTAGRAM FOR ANNOUNCEMENTS RELATING TO NEW FEATURES, TIPS FOR ARTISTS AND LIVE MASTERCLASSES.

JioSaavn Artist Playlists

Once you have access to JioSaavn Artist One you can create artist playlists that will be showcased on your artist profile. These playlists will first need to be created from your user account by logging in at JioSaavn.com after which you can link them and feature them on your artist page. JioSaavn will use your current artist profile photo and create customized playlist artwork for you. The two playlists available are:

Artist Hits Playlist

Essentially a catalog playlist showcasing the artists original music and a way for fans to also find new releases.

Made By Playlist

This is a playlist of music from any artist. It can include music the artist is inspired by, or likes to listen to. This is also a great opportunity to include music by similar artists, featuring them in your playlist. They may even do the same for you in their playlists.

To update these playlists, you just update the version in your user profile at JioSaavn.com and every 24 hours it will update the version on your artist profile.

JioSaavn Artist Profiles

JioSaavn allows verified artists to add a photo, biography and social media links to their artist profile.

Add A Profile Photo

This should be the very first thing you do. All photos will be reviewed before they will show on the app. Adding an artist image shows fans that you have a presence on JioSaavn.

Add Links To Social Media

Adding links to your social media gives fans an opportunity to follow the artist on multiple other platforms. This means that when they are not streaming your music you have other ways to reach them through social media posts. You can add links to Facebook, Twitter, Instagram, YouTube and Wikipedia.

Add A Bio

Biographies can be added to an artist profile but must be emailed to content-inquiries@saavn.com and kept between 200-250 words. You can also share awards and nominations from a Wikipedia page and mention your top 3 songs. These submissions will be reviewed before they are added so please allow time for them to become available.

JioSaavn Shorties

"Shorties" are high quality short videos for songs (similar to Spotify's Canvas). Listeners will be able to watch these videos on loop while listening to a song on the JioSaavn app.

These videos are 3-15 seconds long and play in vertical mode to show on listeners' phones.

JioSaavn Editorial Playlists

Currently the only know way to submit music for editorial playlist consideration is via the contact form located at https://artists.jiosaavn.com.

It is advised to include as much detail about the song as possible. Definitely include detail on Language, Genre, Mood and Instruments used etc. You can also suggest an editorial playlist that you think the song would be a good fit for.

Select a reason

Wrong songs appear in my profile

Few songs are missing from my profile

Spelling change in my displayed artist name

My access request is still pending

I got access to wrong profile

There is an issue with stats on my profile

✓ Pitch my new song for editorial playlist

I have another issue

Bandsintown for Artists

Bandsintown has expanded their online tools. In 2020, the service previously known as Bandsintown Manager was relaunched as Bandsintown for Artists. Bandsintown allows artists to upload tour dates and promote shows to their 50 million registered users as well as promoting across Billboard, Google, Facebook, Instagram, Amazon Alexa and more.

Here's a quick summary of the current features:

- All artists can sign up at artists.bandsintown.com

- Artists on Bandsintown now have the ability to schedule posts to trackers in advance

- Real-time analytics on artist posts

- A daily flow of helpful tips, best practices, and music industry news from Bandsintown's artist resource Hypebot and an expanded Bandsintown For Artists blog

- A curated Artists Services section offering discounts and special offers for artist-focused products and services

Additionally, Bandsintown for Artists has a messaging platform. When a user follows an artist on Bandsintown, they become a "tracker", which means they want to be updated when that artist is performing in their city. This messaging platform allows artists to send emails and push notifications to trackers. In addition, messages can be scheduled and geo-targeted to trackers in a specific location. Artists can also send personalized messages to fans on Bandsintown and sync them across Facebook and Twitter simultaneously.

This messaging service can be used to promote almost anything, not just tour dates. You can share new music releases, merchandise, music videos, secret shows and more.

Social Media and Repurposing Content

Contributed by Nick Ditri

Now more than ever in the history of the internet, it's vital to have a presence on social media. Whether it is a couple pieces of content spread across socials every day or picking your favorite platforms, really push into your engagement. Make them your own. Send fans to that specific platform so they know what you're going to offer. For us, with Disco Fries, our current focus is driving our Twitch streams and further driving our new website FinishMyTrack.com.

In 6 months to a year, those goals could change and likely will, but we always develop a strategy so it works for a term - 3 months, 6 months or a year +. We are strong believers in repurposing content. If we do an interview on Twitch, we will take the best clips and the most reacted to clips from that stream. We will then cut them down, create captions and then share those across our other socials, which are then drivers back to our Twitch stream. We also share these on our website FinishMyTrack.com, which is also the title of our Twitch stream. Our stream drives ultimately to the Finish My Track website for producers and artists to get mixing, mastering and additional production services.

If you think of yourself as the center-of-your-own-universe-brand, whether you are a business or an artist brand, all roads should travel back to YOU in some form or another. Think of your social presence as your tentacles to bring people back to whatever your main focus is, whether that's a track, merch drop or a live activation.

Repurposing content isn't just limited to social content. You can also utilize your song to make multiple pieces of content. Something as simple as taking a lyric or your cover art and making it into canvas art can help engage fans in new ways and create new touch-points for potential fans. You can also take elements of your song - such as unique elements of your vocal, one shots of guitars or synths and any other unique parts that you've created - and develop your own sample pack, which you can then resell. Of course, then you're creating a whole other piece of content you have to get out there and market. Ultimately, you can use one piece of content and stretch it out into almost a month's worth of product, if not more.

One of the biggest and most beneficial uses of socials for us has been engaging with our DMs - whether that's creating a personal connection with fans or reaching out to other artists personally - versus going through managers and agents. Having a personal connection with an artist to create collaboration opportunities is second to none.

Checking our DMs literally changed our career. Tiësto reached out to us over DM. He was supporting our music at the time and reached out to us asking what we were working on. We met up, and he asked us to work on his album! We co-produced his first platinum single in North America called "Wasted" featuring Matthew Koma. If it wasn't for us being engaged in our DMs, that would have never happened.

Never undervalue the idea of personal connection with an artist. Reaching out to people directly while respecting their time and inbox space, no matter if you're signed onto a huge label or you're just an artist on the rise, is meaningful to develop relationships.

Follow Nick and The Disco Fries at <u>finishmytrack.com</u> and @thediscofries on socials.

Create a Great Playlist

Playlists are one of the best ways to discover, share and rediscover music, so it only makes sense to want to have one of your own. Creating a playlist is the first step in creating something of value that you can use as leverage when reaching out to share music with other curators, but first let's make sure you have a great playlist.

You have music. Even if it is just one song, it's a great song and you'd like to see it added to some playlists. The first thing you need to do is to create a playlist that your song will fit into. Choose songs from artists similar to yourself or songs from a specific genre.

Stuck on ideas? Think about:

- Artists that inspired you to write your latest single

- Songs that make you cry

- Songs you listen to while studying

Still stuck? Here's one more. Look up some of your local music venues and see which acts they are booking. After adding a few local artists to your playlists, make sure to reach out to them, letting them know you've added their music. You may find that once local artists begin to share your playlists, their fans may start sharing it as well.

You are a local artist too! There is no shame in adding your own music. Additionally, you are helping others in your own scene, which could lead to things outside of streaming, such as new gig opportunities.

Playlist Curation

Now you should hopefully have a playlist of 50 - 100 songs. Take your time here. Put the strongest songs at the start. If you are doing a pop playlist, put some well-known pop songs in the first ten tracks. Most people decide whether they like a playlist by pressing Play and skipping through the first few songs. After this is when you can take a "risk" and add something the listener may not know, but keeping it relevant and making sure it fits with the rest of the songs on your playlist.

TIP: DID YOU NOTICE I ONLY TOLD YOU TO CREATE ONE PLAYLIST? YOU SHOULD FOCUS YOUR ENERGY ON GROWING THE FOLLOWERS ON ONE TO START WITH. I'VE SEEN ARTISTS MAKE 20-30 PLAYLISTS AND THEN SPEND MOST OF THEIR "STUDIO TIME" KEEPING THEM FRESH. KEEP IT SIMPLE, AND DO ONE PLAYLIST FOR NOW!

Playlist Artwork

Your playlists have to look as good as they sound. People see artwork before they click Play, so boil some coffee and crack those knuckles and let's get designing! If graphic design isn't one of your strengths, here's a tip: Go to a website like Unsplash.com. Services like this enable you to download high resolution images and artwork royalty-free.

Once you have found a few images, go to Canva.com. For someone who has little graphic design experience, this online service is a great place to start. Canva has free templates and text fonts for almost everything. Just drag your image in, change the text to your playlist name and just like that, you look like a professional. If you have a logo, don't forget to include this in your artwork to raise awareness and maintain consistency with your branding.

Playlist Description

This is where you "sell" your playlist to potential new fans. If the description is about all the feels people will be hit with once they press Play, tell that in a brief story in two sentences or less.

It's also essential to include keywords. When you search for anything in Google, you type a few words to make sure you get the most relevant search results at the top. This is the same when searching for playlists on a streaming service. If your playlist contains music spanning five genres, then list all five genres in the description.

For the playlist title, make it something people want to hear and show some personality in it. "Songs I Cry With My Cat To" or "Festival Season Bangers" are clear descriptions of what to expect.

Collaborative Playlists

Most services allow users to create collaborative playlists. When shared, these playlists allow other users to add, remove and change the order of songs in the playlist. This is useful when creating a playlist for your band, as all members can add songs from their own devices. I used this to build the order for my debut album with my band.

Please keep in mind that if these are public, anyone can find them and make changes. Only share the link with trusted people and always make backups of these playlists to avoid losing hours of curation.

TIP: CREATE A SECOND VERSION OF YOUR MOST POPULAR PLAYLIST AS AN ARCHIVE. THIS WILL BE A PERMANENT RECORD OF ALL SONGS YOU HAVE SUPPORTED, ARTISTS CAN DISCOVER THIS LONG AFTER YOU SUPPORTED THEM IN YOUR MAIN PLAYLIST AND THIS WILL DIRECT ARTISTS TO YOUR BRAND.

Playlists on Multiple Services

Don't put all your eggs in one basket. You have a great playlist on Spotify. Why not push that same playlist to YouTube Music, Napster, Pandora, Apple Music, QoBuz, SoundCloud, Deezer and more?

Imagine how much more value your playlist would have if it was on all other primary streaming services. That's why I expanded my Spotify playlists to other DSPs.

It probably sounds like a lot of work, but it isn't! Here are two services that will make your life a lot easier and save you from logging into multiple services each time you want to add a song to your playlist.

TIP: IN THE FIRST EDITION OF THE BOOK, I MENTIONED A SERVICE CALLED SOUNDSGOOD. THIS SERVICE WAS SHUT DOWN IN 2020 DUE TO AN ACQUISITION BY DIGITAL MUSIC DISTRIBUTOR BELIEVE.

Soundiiz

This service has a web-based interface that allows you to automatically synchronize your playlists, including description and song order with adds/removals to multiple platforms.

Soundiiz also creates smart links which can link to your playlist on multiple DSPs. You can even include links to your socials or your submission form. They also provide unique URLs you can share which allow people to log in and stream your playlist on their desired streaming service, even if you don't have a profile set up on that streaming service.

Soundiiz also syncs the playlist order, so if you put a new song at the top of your playlist and remove some songs, it will sync the playlist order across all platforms, currently with the exception of Apple Music. It is worth mentioning that this is only available through a web browser and there is no iOS or Android app available at this time.

Services currently supported:

Soundiiz, Qobuz, Tidal, Last.fm, Spotify, Apple Music, Deezer, YouTube, YouTube Music, Napster, SoundCloud, iTunes, Yandex Music, VK, Setlist.fm, 8Tracks, Pandora, Yousee Musik, JioSaavn, Plex, Slacker Radio, Telmore Musik, Hype Machine, Discogs, Brisamusic, Moodagent, Audiomack, Beatport, Joox, Beatsource, iHeartRadio, KKBox, Idagio, Amazon Music, Playzer, Emby, Claro Música, Dailymotion, Hearthis.at, Sberzvuk, Qub Musique, D'music, SoundMachine, Jamendo, Movistar and BandCamp.

Songshift

SongShift is an iOS app for Apple devices. It offers more streaming services and also boasts an auto sync option (for paid subscribers). Auto sync works well for pushing new songs to playlists. Keep in mind this will only occur when the app is open but you will receive notifications telling you to open the app and sync your new songs. Song positions in playlists don't sync and song removals are not synchronized.

This app is good for a curator who wants to have their music on multiple services and won't ever remove songs from their playlist. I use SongShift to create a permanent back up of every song I have ever added to my main playlist.

Services currently supported:

Spotify, Apple Music, YouTube, SoundCloud, Deezer, Hype Machine, Napster, Pandora, Tidal, Discogs, Last.fm

Grow Your Playlist Following

You have started to get a following on your playlists. People are listening, talking about and sharing your music and playlists. Now it's time to take it to the next level.

When you add a song to your playlist, kindly suggest to the artist that they share your playlist on their social media. In your message, you could have a friendly suggestion saying "Feel free to share the good news on your social media" then include your social links in your signature, so they can tag you.

Don't ever include your personal social media links in your signature, unless you want people hitting you up on your personal profiles.

You can go one step further and have a pre-written Tweet that the artist can copy and paste. This way, you can make sure they tag you correctly use the correct links. Here's an example you can tweak to make your own:

Thanks @askmikewarner for adding me to your New Country playlist. Everyone go follow this playlist and give it a play.

open.spotify.com/playlist/3JNbSnDJWgb3gwUTHigP7f

TIP: SPOTIFY HAS DEVELOPED A GREAT WAY FOR YOU TO SHARE YOUR SPOTIFY INFORMATION BY USING SPECIAL CODES. VISIT SPOTIFYCODES.COM TO FIND OUT ABOUT HOW THESE CODES CAN ENABLE YOU TO SHARE INFORMATION AND CREATE MARKETING MATERIALS.

Post Playlist Artwork

Post playlist artwork on Facebook, Twitter, and Instagram. Tag all new artists whose music you have added that week.

At the very least, you will get a "like". Some artists may even reach out and ask for your email to send you more music. Either way, it is a win/win as you have a new connection.

If you are not constantly changing your artwork, posting the exact same image every week is likely to cause you to lose followers.

Short Links

Use a URL shortener to turn those long URLs into something short and easy to share. Here's a few useful sites.

sptfy.com - Shortens Spotify share links (e.g. sptfy.com/coconutkids links to artist profile)

Bit.ly - Shortens any link. Use for your artist website, a youtube video, social media, anything online (e.g. bit.ly/2H9OQXj links to submission form on Work Hard Playlist Hard website)

toneden.io - Creates a fanlink to share your album, playlist and social media all on one page. Users can choose their favorite streaming service and it will direct them to your profile or playlist on that streaming service automatically (e.g. fanlink.to/datenight links to artist profile on all streaming services).

These services offer a number of added benefits including click tracking, which means you can see how many people followed your link and where they came from. The other benefit of having a short link is for posts on services like Instagram that don't allow clickable links in the photo description. You can type in a short URL that's easy to remember, allowing users to manually type it into their web browser.

Gates

A gate is a way to gift something in return for an action. For example, you can offer a free download of a song, e-book (grin) or something else of value in return for a social action such as following a channel on YouTube, following a playlist on Spotify or sharing a tweet, etc. You can create a gate using services like show.co or toneden.io

You can also create your gate by hiring a developer through a website like Upwork.com. As always, do your research first and make sure your gate complies with the terms and conditions of your relevant streaming service.

TIP: USE A GATE TO GROW YOUR SPOTIFY FOLLOWERS. YOU WILL NOTICE THAT THE MORE FOLLOWERS YOU HAVE, THE HIGHER AMOUNT OF STREAMS WILL COME THROUGH VIA RELEASE RADAR.

Marketing Tools

Streaming services want you to share links to your profile, playlists and music on their platform. They also want you to look good while doing it. Here are the current marketing websites for these streaming services that allow you to create banners, widgets and custom links to share your releases on your website or social media.

Apple Music/iTunes tools.applemusic.com

Deezer developers.deezer.com/musicplugins/player

Spotify developer.spotify.com/technologies/widgets/

Tidal embed.tidal.com

YouTube Music developers.google.com/youtube

Pitch Your Music to Curators

Now that you have value in your own playlists, you might find that other curators become more receptive to your emails. Ask permission before sending music, showing respect from one curator to another. If the curator is also an artist or record label, you can add one of their songs to your playlist as a great ice breaker. Of course, be a good curator and only add music that is a good fit in your playlists.

Think about it. How many times per day do curators receive emails that start with "I'm sure you get a lot of these emails..."? Just stop! You aren't going to stand out if your approach is the same as everyone else. You are reaching out to an artist or label that is also a curator. Open by telling them the following, in this order:

1. You added their song to your playlist. Link.

2. You would like to hear more music from them, invite them to add you to their mailing list or send you new songs directly.

3. That's it.

"I didn't ask them to listen to my music, and I didn't even tell them I'm an artist." That's right - This isn't about you, this is about them! Send a nice email, LinkedIn InMail, or Facebook DM.

If they don't respond within three days, post on Twitter/Facebook, share your playlist publicly and tag the artist, saying something about why you like the song and why everyone needs to hear it. Lastly, mention it was added to your playlist and include a link.

If this doesn't work, repeat for the next single from that artist. Keep doing this. If you add 20 songs by 20 artists you like to your playlist, you may only get one response. Imagine if you add 100 songs to your playlist. That's five new relationships starting to flourish.

Once you have a direct line to the artist, start out by having brief, fun conversations. This will be a relief for them and you may find they will even start writing to you randomly to get something off their chest or to tell you about their fun weekend.

Now that you've built some rapport, send an email with the following in this order.

1. Hey (name), followed by one sentence of friendly banter so they know it's personal.

2. I have added your new song to my playlist, and I've included details below.

3. But first, I've meant to ask if you are open to receive the occasional song submission from me for your playlist consideration. Let me know as I've got a new single coming out that would fit your XXXXXX playlist.

4. Lastly, here's the link to my playlist, I added your track to the top and will share the news on social media today.

Organization Is Key

Once you get a "yes", start building your database. It's important to note the following details.

• Name

• Preferred genres

• Submission lead time (private link before release or spotify uri/url once released)

• Where to submit (do they prefer email, message on Facebook, text etc)

• Link to their playlist profile (You don't want to have to keep asking "Where can I find your XXXXXX playlist".

• Phone (Some curators may ask you to text them).

• City, Country (In case you have travel plans, grow the friendship in person).

Reach Out Via Linkedin

A free trial with LinkedIn gives you InMail credits which lets you message people even if you aren't connected. InMail messages are taken more seriously because you've spent money to send that message so it goes to the top of the recipient's inbox. Search for playlist curator or playlist editor.

TIP: SEARCH FOR INTERNS AT RECORD LABELS/PLAYLIST BRANDS ON LINKEDIN. INTERNS ARE USUALLY FOUND PROUDLY DISPLAYING THEIR JOB TITLE AND EMAIL ADDRESS ON LINKEDIN, WHICH MAKES THEM EASY TO FIND AND INTERACT WITH. THEY TEND TO ALSO BE MORE RESPONSIVE TO INMAIL MESSAGES.

The Narrative

Contributed by Jay Gilbert

One of the most crucial elements to any marketing plan is the narrative.

The narrative is a brief story about the artist, release or song. Simply put, it conveys why anyone should care!

The press release is the obvious way the narrative is communicated to the world but there are so many other ways today including the artist website, socials and it's even required for the Spotify track submission form.

I often ask clients, "If you had thirty seconds in an elevator to tell some important person about your band or release, what would you say?" The entire team; management, label, distributor, publicist etc. should all be on the same page communicating the same narrative.

What makes you special as an artist? What is interesting about the release? Is it aspirational? Is it unusual? Did you overcome adversity? A good narrative can be a powerful tool in getting your message across, gaining attention, publicity and ultimately more fans.

Find out more about Jay at label-logic.net

How to Get Noticed

Contributed by Uberjakd

As a Producer and DJ, I get a lot of people asking me where they should focus if they want to get noticed. Whether it's for gigs or perhaps by a major distributor, here are three key things I tell artists to focus on.

Networking - This is key. You need to meet people and they need to know you exist. First and foremost, they need to know what you are about. Shake hands at gigs, send those emails, ask fellow producers for introductions. Having someone know you is one step closer to working with them.

Fanbase - You need to find your fan base of diehard fans that will wear your logo on a t-shirt, bring their friends to your gigs and sing your praises from the rooftops. It's one thing for you to tell people how good you are but to also have a small army ready to shout about your music and support you will cause others to take notice. This will naturally mean more fans and will eventually get you noticed by bookers, labels and major artists that you could collaborate with. Keep your fans engaged, work out what they want, why they follow you and give it to them ideally daily, weekly or as frequently as possible.

Music - You've already been creating, improving and sharing your music. Now that you've got a network and a fanbase, it's time to share it with them. There is no point making the best music in the world if no one hears it! Don't sit on things too long. Know that the journey is finishing and releasing content/music, not obsessing over one song for months because you feel like it s your "big tune". Trust me, you can never be 100% certain which will be your biggest song, so just put it out and let the people decide!

Find out more about Uberjakd at underjakd.com

Music and Livestreaming

Contributed by Karen Allen

As an early supporter and evangelist for livestreaming, I couldn't be more thrilled to see so many artists discovering it, streaming their music, and finding new audiences. The pandemic is/was certainly a motivator for artists to give it a try, but it's clear that it's a solid long term strategy for independent artists.

My book and course go deep on producing a channel on Twitch and growing audience there, but in reality what I teach could apply towards Facebook, YouTube, Reddit, and even Instagram. The core products you'll use – OBS for production and Streamlabs and StreamElements for interactivity and off-platform monetization with your audience – work on most platforms. In fact, the big takeaway for me from the explosion of musicians livestreaming is that there is not just one way to do it. Artists were activating fanbases and getting discovered by music fans and monetizing in meaningful ways on all the platforms.

Where to stream and what to do there really depends on how much time you have to commit to it and whether you have a fanbase established somewhere already. The bottom line is that building on a new platform takes patience, consistency, and time. You didn't build your Instagram following overnight and it will be the same with whichever platform you choose to stream on. If you don't have a lot of time, then stream where you have the most followers. If you do have time to devote to building on a new platform, I still think that Twitch has the best return on your investment in terms of audience development and monetization.

Let's talk about some of the bigger platforms with livestreaming.

Twitch

Music was a growth category on Twitch before the pandemic and has absolutely exploded since. It may seem like it's saturated now, but I hear from artists that they are still able to join and successfully build channels.

You'll start as a Community member (no monetization, but you can livestream) and work your way up to Affiliate. Once you have 50 followers, at least 3 average concurrent viewers, and a minimum number of streams under your belt, you'll become an Affiliate and can charge subscriptions for your channel, viewers can give you Bits (virtual currency), and viewers can earn Points by watching, subbing, and generally participating in your stream. You can determine what viewers earn with Points. You can also design your own emoji (called "emotes") that viewers can use in your channel's chat and in others. This is an important tool for branding and communicating with your audience, as the chat is the main way you'll "talk" with your viewers and create community.

The next step is Partner. It takes a lot of time and growth metrics to earn Partner, and it's not even guaranteed when you hit them. The main benefit of becoming a partner is you get more emotes and Twitch may offer promotional support. It's nice to get, but you certainly don't need it to do well on Twitch.

Pro tip: if you are a reasonably established artist with a good-sized following, have your management contact Twitch to see if they can fast track you to Affiliate or Partner or even pay you to stream. Twitch does paid content deals with artists who can commit to around 25 hours of streaming per month and bring their audience to Twitch.

To meaningfully build audience and earn revenue on Twitch as an indie artist, you'll need to stream at least 3-5 days a week, 2-4 hours per stream. The artists I've seen really grow on Twitch will stream a minimum of 15-20 hours per week. Don't panic! It's not all performance. You'll typically get through a half dozen or so songs per hour because you'll be spending time reading the chat and responding to the audience. This is super important because Twitch is not just a content platform, it's a community platform. What you're really doing is creating a space where people like to hang out, and you are the ring leader of that space.

It's incredibly important to get to know the other streamers and support them. Music streamers on Twitch are great at "coopetition" – they will watch other streamers, subscribe to them, and even "raid" them when their stream is over (sending all your audience into another stream at once) and in turn those streamers will support them back. The music streamer community is very authentic and organic. It's important that you find other streamers you genuinely like, watch their streams, and become a part of their communities. Fakeness and self-promotion is really obvious and icky on Twitch. Look for other streamers you like who you also think you'd share audience with; for example, if they raided you or you raided them, would at least half of the raiders stick around for an hour? That's a successful raid.

Another secret to growth on Twitch is Discord. Discord is a separate platform from Twitch that a lot of streamers use to talk with their fans between streams. You'll set up a server (it's free!) on Discord and invite fans to join your server, where you'll create a bunch of message boards on various topics. You can even create voice and video channels where you can talk or video conference with fans. Join the Discords of other streamers to see how they use it and to get to know them and their communities better.

Twitch is A LOT, right?? If that's all too much, then pick a platform where you already have audience and stream there.

Facebook

Facebook is getting better with livestreaming. Their monetization tools (Stars is their virtual currency) are improving and they have ticketed livestreams now, too. You'll need a Business page that's enabled for paid livestreams. You can check for eligibility in your Creator Studio.

Facebook is great because people can set reminders for your upcoming streams and share your stream while you are live. That's really powerful. If you don't have Stars enabled on your Page, then you can point people to your Venmo or Paypal. Just keep an eye on incoming tips so you can thank people on stream.

You can use OBS to stream to Facebook or use their tools. I recommend OBS. You'll have more control over everything and can use Streamlabs or StreamElements to build in on-screen alerts when people like, share, tip, etc.

YouTube

YouTube is fine if you have a lot of audience there, but I don't find that YouTube is as good as Facebook when it comes to alerting your audience that you're live and viewers certainly can't share the stream within YouTube. YouTube's general directory of streams live now is hard to find and pretty sparse. You'll likely not get on it and have to promote the stream on your own.

YouTube has a few options for monetization – Subscriptions ("memberships"), Super Chat (pinning a chat comment to the top of the chat), and Super Stickers (emoji). You have to qualify for each of these and it's not easy unless your channel already has a lot of subscribers and views.

If you are doing a video premiere on YouTube, I'd recommend doing a livestream there beforehand to generate excitement for it. You can even set up your stream to send all the viewers into the video premiere once the stream is over. It's kind of buried way down in the livestream setup options. Schedule a stream with YouTube Studio, then go to the Content tab on YouTube Studio, click Live, then click your scheduled stream, and scroll down and click Show More to see all the advanced settings.

You can stream directly from YouTube Studio but I recommend you use OBS so you have more control over your visual presentation and can add in features from Streamlabs and StreamElements.

Instagram

Instagram will only show your stream to your followers. There is no way to promote a stream in advance other than making a regular post. If you stream from your phone, I really recommend getting an iRig or similar device so you can connect your audio interface directly and not have to rely on your phone's mic.

There is some monetization on Instagram but it's minimal. The chat flies by fast and can be hard to keep track of. In general, I'm not a big fan of livestreaming on Instagram but if you have a lot of audience there, then it's worth it to have that direct touchpoint with them.

You can use OBS to stream to Instagram! Use a service like Yellowduck.tv. You'll lose some functions, like it won't save your stream to IGTV, but you can save the stream to your computer and upload it later manually.

TikTok

TikTok also will only show your stream to your followers. Because it's phone only, you have some of the same limitations as Instagram in terms of sound quality and reading the chat. TikTok has monetization and can be a lot of fun. You need at least 1000 followers to livestream on TikTok. If you're doing well on that platform, start livestreaming there and get to know your fans.

Reddit

Reddit is the weird dark horse of livestreaming platforms. There is no monetization, but there are not that many people streaming on it so it's not that hard to get audience if you're consistent and the audiences can be in the thousands – way more than you'd get on Twitch with the same amount of effort. If you post your Venmo or Paypal, you're likely to get tips.

You'll either go live from your phone using the Reddit app or go live from your desktop using RPAN (Reddit Public Access Network). RPAN is a free software download and works a lot like OBS. You can find out how to livestream on Reddit at https://www.reddit.com/r/pan/wiki/index.

Ticketed Platforms

There are so many options for ticketed livestream platforms and they are constantly changing, so I won't go through them here. In general, I recommend you do free livestreaming on one of the platforms mentioned above and save the paid streams for special events. The point of livestreaming is to build community, to make watching you perform a habit for your fans, and to provide a place for your fans to hang out with each other. Free is just a better day-to-day strategy for that than ticketed.

Find out more about Karen at **twitchformusicians.com**

Use Your Phone as a Webcam

Many of us are "going live" right now. Whether it is hosting webinars, performing, gaming, attending meetings or simply chatting. Let's be real. the webcam on most of our computers sucks and the quality just doesn't cut it.

While recording a bunch of videos for my online course I realized that the quality from my webcam on my old MacBook was quite poor, not to mention that there were issues with audio sync and lighting. I ended up using my phone to record, using the flash for additional lighting. This led to much higher quality videos.

This got me thinking. If phones have significantly higher quality cameras than our computers, why can't we use our phone as a webcam? So I started searching.

It turns out that if you do have a phone kicking around, even an older phone that perhaps you don't use anymore, you can use it as a webcam. It's as easy as connecting it to your computer and downloading a free app.

The app that I found and I now use in place of my webcam is called Camo. They have a free version, which is what I currently use. The free version provides 720p resolution and simply requires downloading the app onto your PC or Mac and iPhone (Android coming soon), then connecting the two with a Lightning to USB cord (even a third party cable works).

I have tested this with Twitch Studio, Zoom, StreamYard, Google Meet and a handful of other livestream products and it works effortlessly. The video quality is so good that I actually sold my Logitech Brio and now use my iPhone X as my Webcam. What's really cool is that if you have multiple old iPads or iPhones lying around, you can connect them all and essentially change between different "cameras". It looks great, and it's also an awesome way to find a new use for those old devices.

My hope by sharing this information is to help anyone that has been hesitant to go live due to the quality of their existing setup and help them start streaming.

Find Curators Using Chartmetric

Chartmetric lets you sift through almost every playlist/curator on Spotify, Apple Music, Amazon Music, YouTube Music and Deezer. You can also filter out editorial playlists, only seeing independent third party playlists. You can even filter to only see curators who have added their social media URLs, making it easier to narrow down your search to people who are easier to contact.

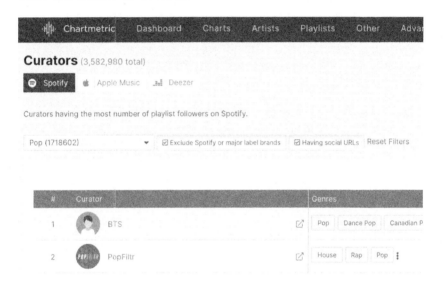

TIP: WHEN REACHING OUT TO A CURATOR, DO NOT INCLUDE ANY SONG LINKS IN YOUR MESSAGE. ASK THEM IF THEY HAVE A SUBMISSION PROCESS. IF THEY RESPOND, THANK THEM AND FOLLOW THEIR INSTRUCTIONS. THIS WILL EARN YOU INSTANT RESPECT FROM THE CURATOR BECAUSE YOU ASKED THEM HOW TO SUBMIT MUSIC TO THEM INSTEAD OF COLD PITCHING, UNLIKE EVERYONE ELSE. ASK PERMISSION, SHOW RESPECT, SAY THANK YOU.

Pitch Via Your Distributor

Pitching your music correctly is a fine art that takes time to master. The good thing is that you are not alone. Here's one method for getting your music in the front of editorial teams at streaming services.

While this information may not be in big neon lettering on your distributor's website, you may find through some research (or by flat-out asking them) that your distributor has contacts at most major streaming services they pitch to. Now, why wouldn't distributors advertise that they have these connections? Because they have thousands of new releases uploaded every week. If they offered this as a service on their front page, every artist would send them a pitch. This is why you have the upper hand. You are educated, you have great music and you are prepared.

Now, approaching your distributor is the same as approaching a curator. Don't hit them with a pitch! Ask if they have a submission process for consideration of upcoming releases to forward to their editorial team contacts at streaming services.

Important things to keep in mind:

— Distributors get lots of direct emails so be patient and give them a few days before following up.

— If you still don't get a reply, try another contact method, look for their artist/label relations contacts on LinkedIn and reach out with a brief, friendly message.

Distributors need lead time, just like editorial teams at major streaming services. Give at least four weeks minimum before your release date. If your song comes out April 29th, you should email them in mid March to be safe.

Paid Pitching Services

If you don't have the time or need a break from pitching, there are a number of services that will do the job for you. These services vary in price and offering. *Do not take these as endorsements.* The services provided are subject to change without notice. Instead, consider this as an outline of the kinds of services that are available.

Playlist Push: This service is extremely detailed in comparison to others, but it comes at a premium price for larger campaigns. Playlist Push actively removes playlists with low monthly listeners and also bans "bot" playlists that have large follower counts but no listeners. A nice touch here is that curators are given a Follow button and encouraged to follow artists whose music they like. The process to add a song is easy and curators may be more likely to add due to how simple it is. They also have an option for TikTok campaigns.

SubmitHub: A service that was created by Jason Grishkoff, who runs a blog called IndieShuffle. SubmitHub allows you to pitch to independent Spotify playlist curators, blogs and YouTube channels. If you get stuck, there is a live chat room on the site with artists, curators and SubmitHub staff available to answer your questions. There are both free and premium submission options, which are achieved by purchasing credits. For premium submissions, if a submitter does not receive a response within 48 hours, a refund in the form of submission credit is honored.

Playlist Pluggers

There is an extremely large number of "playlist pluggers" and "Spotify PR" companies out there. Do your research, ask to see songs they've recently worked on and ask those artists for real feedback. It's common for an artist or label to pay multiple playlist pluggers and then only continue to work with the good ones.

If something sounds too good to be true, it probably is! A few warning signs to look out for include free email accounts (@gmail, etc.) and/or no traceback to any team members on the website. You can also look them up on LinkedIn to see if they have real people working for them. Check out their public page on Facebook, see if any of your friends like the page, then ask them if they have used their services.

Lastly, you can comment on sites such as Reddit (an online forum), asking if anyone has used them before. If people have had a bad experience, they will gladly speak up to save someone else from being ripped off.

Hype Machine

Hype Machine has been around since 2005 and is still referred to by many of my colleagues as their "go to" for finding new music that has yet to hit streaming services. Hype Machine rankings pull data from hundreds of active music blogs and formulates it into charts. All songs are embedded from SoundCloud links, which means artists can upload music to SoundCloud even before it is released, allowing for a blog to "premiere" the song.

It's also a little known fact that some editorial team members at streaming services also subscribe to various music blogs and look to Hype Machine to find new artists that need to be discovered. Personally, I have seen a few artists charting on Hype Machine who are then added to popular discovery playlists such as "Fresh Finds" the following week. While this isn't a guarantee, it's safe to say that being on Hype Machine will at least increase your chances of the right people hearing your music.

Uniquely, being listed on Hype Machine is not achieved by sending them a pitch. The only way for your song to appear on the site is for one of these blogs to write about your song - https://hypem.com/sites.

If you're up for it, you can go through the above list and work through every single blog, contacting them individually and trying to get them to check out your song. Keep in mind that there are many artists using the same method, so for every 200 emails you send, you may get 5 responses and possibly only one blog feature. If this isn't soul-crushing for you, then I highly recommend taking the time to do so.

In SubmitHub, you also have the option to filter the blogs, by genre, as well as only seeing blogs that are on Hype Machine. This means that you are now only focusing on blogs that could get you added to Hype Machine (if they write about your music).

YouTube Channels Can Grow Your Followers

There are some brands on YouTube with millions of followers. These channels are the result of one single curator, or a team of curators spending countless hours sourcing amazing music, engaging with their audience and building an organic following. These channels have built a large amount of trust through uploading great music. It's no surprise that many of these YouTube channels have ventured into the world of record labels.

Since these YouTube channels are launching their own record labels, it makes sense that they are building a following on music streaming services, especially with their own playlists. There are two ways that YouTube channels are promoting their playlists and your profile.

Description

In the description under the visuals, you may see links to the channel's Spotify playlist, the artist's profile and social media.

Gates

Many of these YouTube channels will also offer a free download of a song and include their playlist in the gate. Ask them nicely if they can also add your streaming link in the gate. Given that the free download recipient has already decided that they want your song and they like the channel they discovered it on, following you on a music streaming service should not be an issue. They get free music, you get a new fan, and the channel builds their following on another service.

Making Contact

Best methods for contacting YouTube channel owners can vary. Here are some suggestions on how to make first contact.

• In the About page on the YouTube channel, there will be a button to "view email address" if they've chosen to list it.

• Locate the Facebook fan page for the channel. If they are open to receiving messages, you can reach them here.

• If the channel owner has a Twitter account with open DMs, you can also try messaging them here.

• LinkedIn - InMail message

• SubmitHub - free or paid submission

Before reaching out, take a look at the curator's profile to see if they mention a submission process. If they say, "only submissions through email will be accepted", respect their wishes. Don't slide into their DMs on Twitter.

Make Money as a Curator

If you already have a playlist with a following, people are probably reaching out to you on social media or emailing you their music. Why not make some money, ethically, while you are listening through these submissions? Below are a list of websites that welcome curators to sign up and pay you for listening to submissions and giving constructive, useful feedback.

SubmitHub: Having both a free and premium option, this credit-based service allows submitters to choose specific curators to send their music to. As a curator, you get paid for listening to every premium submission and providing feedback within 48 hours.

Playlist Push: For a varying fee, based on genre and number of curators reached, Playlist Push offers paid campaigns for artist releases. Curators then have two weeks to respond and are monitored heavily to make sure their playlists have engaged listeners. Curators are rewarded a higher payout per submission review based on their following, engaged listeners, feedback value and how long they leave a song in their playlist. Playlist Push also allows TikTok creators to sign up and get paid to create TikTok content,

SoundMachine: A background music service company supplying music to major fashion, hotel, restaurant, and coffee shop chains as well as small businesses. Curators can sign up and make their playlists available for use in real brick-and-mortar stores and get paid for their efforts. Artists featured in their playlists also see potential exposure and income from in-store airplay. Curators can sign up at sound-machine.com/registermusiccurator to find out more.

Be aware of websites that suggest you take payment to guarantee adding a song. This is playola. Just don't do it. We'll get into more detail in the Payola vs Playola chapter.

Creating a Good Playlist

Contributed by Luk

In my opinion, the best way to attract an audience to your playlist is to find a niche that is not heavily saturated. A few years back, this was the case with TikTok-themed playlists but now it seems everyone is creating a "TikTok Hits" playlist.

If you create something that has already been done, you will find it far more challenging to get people to listen and follow your playlist with so much competition out there.

You should choose a specific theme that you would like to curate for. It can be a special type of event or even a mood. Do not find a playlist already in your theme and just copy the track list. You will not get anyone coming to your playlist if yours is just a duplicate of someone else's.

It's understandable that you'll want to add a lot of popular songs already on the radio or doing well on streaming. That being said, you should also use this opportunity to insert some songs from lesser-known artists to give them an opportunity to get heard. Not only is this beneficial to the artist, but it's also great for the listener as you are helping them discover new music.

It's important not to use long or extended versions of songs. Any song with a long intro or outro can cause people to skip that song or, even worse, skip your playlist and start listening to another one. People bore easily.

Do not buy any followers. People see right through this, and it will impact your ranking on Spotify. You risk your playlist getting removed from Spotify and having to start all over again with zero followers.

Artwork is important. Before people even press play, they will look at the artwork. If it's not attractive to them, they may move on to the next playlist.

Tell people about your playlist on social media. Share updates when you make a significant update to the playlist, and tell other artists when you add them so they can share the good news.

In addition to being a playlist curator, I am also an artist. By creating my own playlists, I know that when I release music I will always have a good home for it alongside the relevant playlists that I own. This also led me to create my own online community at songrocket.com where other curators, artists and labels can connect with each other.

Find out more about Luk at _songrocket.com_

The Power of E-Mail

Contributed by Cheryl B. Engelhardt

While you've got some work to do claiming accounts, pitching to curators and the like, there's also a whole other avenue we can go down - your fans. More specifically, your fan list (email list).

People are *three* times as likely to click on a link in an email than on social media, which makes your email list prime real estate for sharing your artist streaming links and letting your fans make a dent in your streaming numbers for you.

Here are a few strategies, specifically around using your email list (no matter how big or small!) to utilize the great stuff in this book:

Pro Email Tips

1. Stick to short and sweet, curiosity-invoking subject lines. Leave the rest for the body of the email. The job of the subject line is to get them to *open* the email.

2. Once they've opened, make sure you are only asking them to do one thing. Send them to *one* link. Talk about *one* platform you want them to follow you on. Make sure that *one* link appears several places throughout the email, including in the first part of the email so they don't have to scroll to find it. Adding in an image that goes to your link as well as a button, if your email provider allows for that, are also great spots to have the link. I like to see four placements of your link.

3. Don't be afraid to send more than one email in a week about the same thing. You can change up the context. For example, if you are using the week to focus on Spotify, invite people to follow you in the first email and explain that your new music will end up in their Release Radar. The second email can be an invitation to listen to a specific song. If you have a song that would be good to listen to on a weekend -

perhaps an upbeat, let-your-hair-down type song - send it out on a Friday and encourage your audience to listen over the weekend!

4. If you don't have a list yet or don't know where to start, that's okay. Just watch a couple of videos on your chosen email platform (more below on this) just so you can have a place to legally collect emails from people who want to hear from you! The best email platform for you is the one *you* will master and use.

If it seems overwhelming to send even one newsletter a year, don't stress. I got you!

First off, let's delete "newsletter" from our vocabulary. Newsletters are outdated and ineffective, mostly because we are now in a world where social media has conditioned us to expect the one-topic-post. We see a photo, there's a caption about that photo, and on we go. Email is the same idea - You may have many things to say and that's fine, but if you have different calls to action, then the best course of action is to split up those topics to different emails. Focus is your friend when it comes to email marketing. (See #2 above).

Here's a step-by-step way to look at email. We'll zoom out and look at the big picture, then get into the logistics and tech. Finally, we'll tackle how to grow email lists, engage and eventually monetize them.

Let's think about email in S.T.A.G.E.S. (Such a good acronym for musicians, right?)

Strategy: W*hy* do you want an email list? How do you think connecting with your fans regularly will support your career? If you don't know the answer to this, any email you send will feel like you're throwing spaghetti at the wall and seeing what sticks. This isn't a stage that needs tons of time to figure out: **A strategy isn't a fancy long business plan. It's knowing what you want and then choosing actions to get you there.** Which leads into the next stage:

Technology: The tech of running a smooth and easy email list can be a major block for a lot of us, but with just a few minutes on Youtube after choosing your platform, you can be up and running. Your email platform is the program you use to bring in new subscribers and automate sending consistent content and updates. I recommend Kajabi for an all-inclusive experience. Mailchimp, Active Campaign and Mailerlite are also great, but there are dozens more to choose from. Again, the best email platform for you is the one you will master and use!

Attracting: This is the stage where your tech is fully set up, and you are ready to attract the right people. In this stage, you're thinking about *how* you talk about your email list and *where* you will talk about it. Do you offer a free bundle of songs in exchange for an email? A discount code to your merch store? I like to give subscribers something when the first sign up. It's a gesture that says "I value your email and that you are giving it to me. Here's a gift in exchange." Don't get hung up on what you're giving them. Remember, it's the gesture that counts. Just make sure this thing is easily consumable - as in, not an entire book or an hour-long video.

Once you have your submission form up and running on a page that explains what people are receiving when they sign up, it's time to put that link everywhere, including:

- Your email signature

- Your about sections and bios in social media profiles

- In the description and comments section of every live stream you do.

And of course, talk about it in person and on any live videos or performances you do! People won't know about your email list until they hear about it.

Growth: This is the area that can cause another big block - once you've got your friends and family on your list, then what? How do you expand beyond your own world on social media to grow that mailing list? There are many ways to do this but for now, I'll focus on three:

The first is to cross-promote with other musicians that also have mailing lists. You can each send an email to your own lists saying something like "Oh hey, I met this great musician and they're giving away one of their songs - here's the link to go grab it." As long as you know they have a great email list system going, you're providing your subscribers with great content and the other artist is doing the same, while simultaneously sending new potential fans your way.

The second way is to run ads. This is a whole other marketing beast but ads on facebook, instagram and audio ads on Spotify directing people to a short link (a link easy to remember and say) that allows them to sign up is a great way to go.

The last way I like to expand my list is through brand partnerships. This can be with a venue you're playing at, through a brand you use or a gear company you're connected to. Making a request to highlight your free offer in exchange for whatever they need is a great place to start.

Engagement: Once you've got people heading to your signup form and subscribing, this one key point is important to remember: New people on your list are not necessarily fans. They are subscribers. It is your job, through your email content, to turn them into fans. This is what engagement is all about.

I'm a big fan of automation - emails that go out automatically based on a subscriber's behavior. This is a great system to get set up because you don't have to stress every month about sending that "newsletter" or broadcast. Your subscribers will be taken along a journey with you, even if you get kidnapped by aliens. Cool!

The most important thing is to have a great welcome series set up so you can easily set up expectations and give them great content to keep them on your list for the long haul. Then you can set up a nurture series (emails that tell stories and get them interested in your journey and your craft). Be clear on what you're selling and when you will sell it. (I call these RISE series.)

It takes a little bit of time to get organized, get outlines, and get writing to all of these series are set up, but once they are, you're rolling in email magic.

Selling: Monetizing your list and even promoting your music and streaming sites are all things you want to tackle in this stage of email. Promotion may not necessarily mean you're selling something. For example, creating a series of emails around following you on Instagram or Spotify will have a similar strategy to encouraging people to pre-order a new album: there is something important to you that will help you accomplish a goal, and you have a specific action you'd like the reader to take. These emails are different from nurture emails, where you're sharing stories of your journey and there isn't necessarily an action to take.

We don't want to cause promotion fatigue, when we are *always* asking our fans to do something. This is why we want to be clear on our goal and the ONE main action we need them to take to help us get there.

Email is one of the most underutilized tools in a musician's tool box, and the data shows it's not going anywhere soon. If you're just starting out, it's a perfect time to start an email list and bring people in on your music career growth. If you've got bunches of music released, SWEET, you've got tons of content waiting to be shared with your future subscribers. If you have an established email list, even better. Figure out which area of playlisting you want to focus on first, and bring your fans into that part of your music career. Tell them why it's important to you. They're going to want to get on board and help you.

The worst thing a musician can do is to tell their fans about their big goal but not have a response to "How can I help?". Be ready with your specific call to action, and be ready to yell it from the rooftops. Or at least through an email.

Find out more about Cheryl at inthekeyofsuccess.com

Why Your Pitches Aren't Working

Ever wondered why your email pitches aren't receiving a positive response, or any response at all? These are examples of real emails that have been sent to real people.

You Don't Include A Link

Hey . I just put out a new track on my YouTube.
It will great if you can show some support, like , comment, subscribe or maybe give some feedback.
Thanks

Sent from Yahoo Mail on Android

If people have to do ANY additional work to find your song, you've already lost. If they are already reading your email, include a link and make it easy for them.

This is, of course, under the assumption you have already emailed the receiver before. I always advise artists to not send links in the first email. Instead, ask permission to send music and ask the curator if they have a submission process. If you follow their process and respect their inbox you may find you have more success getting music noticed by them in future.

You CC Multiple People

If you are pushing for a blog premiere and telling someone that you sent them your track first because they are special, send them an individual and personal email. If they are cc-ed, it's obvious they are not the only recipient. It's impossible to feel "special" when you are one of 100 recipients. You've also just shared a list of email addresses that may be personal and will no doubt see a large amount of spam if it gets into the wrong hands.

Small Talk

Hello Dear

hope all is well? Hows the weather treating you?
I was wondering if you listened to ████████ songs yet ?

What if the recipient is ill or dealing with a personal crisis? They could even be in an area dealing with a flood or extreme weather. This can come across as inconsiderate. Avoid small talk like asking someone how their family or their health is. That's fine if you are already friends, but it's a little awkward in cold outreach and follow up emails. Getting to the point and skipping past the small talk allows the reader to get to your music quicker and increase the chances of them clicking and listening.

You Attach Files

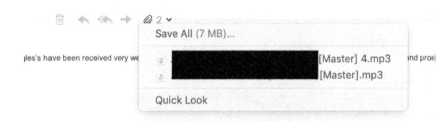

We aren't all blessed with high speed, unlimited data or lots of storage on our devices for emails. By attaching an MP3 file or (yikes) movie, you are forcing that recipient to download your song without giving them a choice. This slows down their email and will likely lead to your email being deleted once it has finished downloading. I personally know people who block emails with large attachments, meaning your email may ever even make it to their inbox.

A streaming link with downloads enabled is far more acceptable. This can be a SoundCloud or DropBox link where the recipient can click, stream and download if they choose too.

You Tell Them Where To Place Your Song

You have to add this to your Fashion Store Sounds playlist, it's the perfect fit.

Curators will make their decision themselves. This can be taken as an insult by telling them where to place your song. At the very least, it's rude. Let them listen and decide if and where it fits. Your goal is just to get them to listen.

What Curators Look For

A common question I see on social media is "How do you choose which music goes into your playlists?". I've seen this question asked many times online and I want to share my answer with you.

I can't speak for everyone, but for me it's all about personal taste. For myself as a curator, choosing music comes down to a few things:

— Production quality. Is it mastered? Does it sound good when played alongside the other songs in the playlist?

— Is it a good song? Is there something that makes it stand out, whether it's well written, features an amazing vocalist, or has a great story?

— Will it fit one of my current playlists? If a song is in a totally different genre to other songs, it can't be added.

— Explicit content. While I am ok with adding songs with explicit content on some playlists, this can be a deal breaker for some curators. Consider having a clean version of your song available as an alternative. Your distributor should be able to set this up for you.

I listen to all music in the order it is submitted. Personally, I don't read press kits, bios, or even look up the artist on social media. I don't care if an artist has 100 streams or 1 million streams. If I like the song, I will add it.

TIP: IT'S WORTH NOTING THAT SINCE THE FIRST EDITION OF *WORK HARD PLAYLIST HARD*, I HAVE STEPPED AWAY FROM PLAYLIST CURATION. MY FOCUS NOW IS ON EDUCATING ARTISTS THROUGH THIS BOOK AND GROWING OUR ONLINE COMMUNITY AT WORKHARDPLAYLISTHARD.COM

Create a Release Spreadsheet

Contributed by Kelli-Leigh

No matter what point you are at with your music, it's never too late to get organized. Make a spreadsheet of your catalogue that includes all of the key information about every song you've created. It will save you a lot of time and energy in the future.

Let's say that you change distributors one day. You'll need to transfer over your catalogue to a new distributor and they would need all ISRC & UPC codes. You can also include links to the release (song files, artwork, notes) in the spreadsheet as well. Having an up-to-date spreadsheet that lists every release, product code and creator information (writers & contributors), will keep you a step ahead when needing to reference your data.

Connect with Kelli-Leigh at _kelli-leigh.com_

Branding and Identity

Contributed by Ryden

Branding encompasses everything from your musical signature to your visual aesthetic. It's a key part of your strategy that will help you stand out. Visually and sonically, your music should look and feel like *you*.

Who is this "you"? It should start with the music. By now, you've probably locked in on a certain style of music you like to make. If you haven't, give yourself plenty of time. This is a big decision that will determine your path, genre and even your industry. You'll need to examine your influences, find out what you're passionate about and experiment hundreds of times to see what really vibes with you. Then, if you're like me, you'll probably release some music and change your mind all over again.

Once you've figured out your sonic brand, move on to your visual identity. This can include everything from your fashion style and color palette to your social media look and logo. It should help bring your music to life. As needed, bring people on board at this stage to help illustrate your vision. A good logo designer, graphic artist, photographer and even a stylist will take you a long way.

Finally, a much more elusive part of your brand will be your messaging. Do some soul searching. Maybe do a lot. What do you stand for? What do you believe in? What do you want your music to make people feel? Your messaging can translate to moving love songs (John Legend, Sam Smith), heartrending angst (Billie Eilish, Olivia Rodrigo), female empowerment (Beyonce, Christina, Pink), social initiatives (Nipsey Hussle, Kendrick, Common) or just straight-up party vibes (LMFAO, early Ke$ha). Anything goes, but be clear on what's going.

Figure out who you are, and then let your art tell the story.

Connect with Ryden on socials @OfficialRyden.

Protect Yourself

Now that you are growing - whether as an artist, curator, or both - you have something of value in your fans, followers and your brand. You need to protect your social media profiles from hungry hackers who want to take over your fan page or delete your account. Unfortunately, there are shady people out there. Don't panic though, there are plenty of things you can do to make sure you protect all of your accounts. Follow these steps.

Passwords

Change your passwords yearly and never use the same password again. Use a different password for each site. If someone gets your Facebook password and it also happens to be the same password for your internet banking, you can find yourself in a world of trouble.

Don't save passwords in online documents. Just assume that nothing stored online is safe. Buy a notebook, write them all down, and put that notebook in your safe!

Use long passwords. Hackers use bots to cycle through password combinations until they guess your password. The longer your password, the longer it will take them to guess, and by then you will have already changed your password.

Two factor authentication is an extra layer of security. In addition to entering your password, a short temporary password is sent to your phone and is also required to be entered before you can log in to your account.

App / Website Logins

Remember all those websites that allow you to login with your Facebook account? Well, if someone hacks into your Facebook, guess what they also have access to?

This also applies to Google and other accounts. Whatever platform you use, search the Help Center and find out how to remove unnecessary third party logins/apps that have access to your account.

Create Music for Playlists

Curators add songs that fit into their playlists. The song must match a specific feel, genre, or style with the rest of the songs. Think about radio edits of songs: they are short and to the point. This is for time management and to keep the audience from changing stations. The same principle applies to playlists. This is why it is important to release a short version of your song specifically catered for playlists.

Before we proceed, please don't let this ruin your creativity or originality. Finish the original unmodified version as intended and then work on a short edit that is geared towards fitting into playlists. Make a short version that will fit in popular playlists with other short songs or radio edits.

Look at popular playlists on Spotify with similar music to what you are releasing. Listen to them, and take note of the following:

— Song length (Under 4 minutes)

— Intro length (Less than 15 seconds, or people may skip before the 30 second mark)

— Outro length (Less than 15 seconds, so people let your song play all the way through)

— Song structure (Start with the main hook, vocal, or something that lets people know what your song is about in the first 15 seconds). **Playing a song only counts as a stream if people listen for more than 30 seconds.** If they listen to your song for less than 30 seconds, it doesn't count and you don't get paid. You need to grab their attention early so they don't skip, then hold their attention at least past the first 30 seconds (and hopefully for the rest of the song).

This will give you an idea of what to do for your edit. Again, don't let this ruin your creativity. Finish your song first, then make an edit. You can include both versions by releasing the radio edit first as a single, then save the extended version (with your epic intro) for the album.

TIP: IF YOU HAVE A REALLY LONG INTRO FOR YOUR SONG, MAKE IT INTO A SEPARATE TRACK. THIS WAY, IF SOMEONE SKIPS THE INTRO, YOUR "REAL" SONG WILL PLAY NEXT. IF THEY LISTEN THROUGH YOUR INTRO TO YOUR MAIN SONG, YOU GET TWO SEPARATE STREAMS TALLIED. FOR AN EXAMPLE OF THIS, CHECK OUT DATE NIGHT'S SELF-TITLED ALBUM HTTPS://OPEN.SPOTIFY.COM/ALBUM/2OQQQSUV2IKYFUDXN8YWRM. KEEP IN MIND THAT FOR AN INTRO OR INTERLUDE TRACK TO ALSO GENERATE STREAMING REVENUE, IT MUST BE AT LEAST 30 SECONDS LONG.

It's one thing to create a short version of your song. It's another to create music specifically for curators to potentially make a living strictly from being on playlists. There's no right or wrong, but the latter can be a huge blow to creativity. For some artists with a very niche market, however, this may be worth trying out.

Let's take Lance Allen for example. Lance is an extremely talented guitarist and has built a large following through his beautiful guitar covers and acoustic original productions. Initially, he got lucky with the Spotify algorithms, but this wasn't enough for Lance.

Instead of sitting on his hands to wait and see if Spotify would support his newest single, Lance decided to approach independent curators with large followings himself. His next step, however, was pure genius. Lance didn't pitch his song to the curators. Instead, he asked them what they were looking for when considering song additions! This is the best way to get a curators attention. Instead of telling them what you want, you're asking them what they are looking for.

Let's say that Curator A responds with "I'm looking for an acoustic cover of the new Bruno Mars song. I love the song, but my playlist is strictly acoustic covers". Lance can then go and record this, knowing that once the song is created there is a very good chance this curator will be adding it to their playlist, especially knowing it was created specifically for them.

Yes, Lance is a guitarist but this can apply to a singer/songwriters, bands and even someone that can play one heck of a pan flute. If you have a niche audience, I am sure these curators would love to hear from you while supporting your releases.

There are many benefits to collaborating with additional artists on a song. You can achieve a different sound or simply bring on a guest vocalist. The result can be unique and potentially loved by both your audience and theirs.

The best part of this comes when releasing your music. Not only will the song reach your audience, it will also reach theirs. If you have 1,000 followers on Spotify and they have 1,000 followers, you have potentially doubled your audience for the track.

To make sure you reach all followers, you need to have both artists as a "main artist". If you have one artist as "featuring", it won't reach their audience through the likes of Release Radar or necessarily show on their profile as one of their latest releases. In short, it may be buried further down on their artist profile. As another bonus, all main artists will have the opportunity to submit the song through Spotify for Artists.

TIP: YOU CAN CURRENTLY INCLUDE UP TO 5 ARTISTS AS A "MAIN ARTIST" BEFORE THE ARTIST NAME WILL SWITCH TO "VARIOUS ARTISTS".

If all artists involved are actively promoting, sharing and pitching the release you have increased your chances significantly.

If you start a new project under a new alias, or a collaboration, you don't have to lose your followers. One example is Diplo and Mark Ronson. Both have huge follower counts. They started a project called Silk City (which had no followers initially). Their debut single had four main artists tagged Silk City, Diplo, Mark Ronson and Dua Lipa. This meant that the debut single from their new project would reach all of the combined followers for the four artist profiles. With a combined follower count in the millions and guaranteed Release Radar placement if submitting more than

7 days prior to release, this makes for a successful release, regardless of what additional support they receive.

Contributed by Andee Connors

Whatever your art is - music, comedy, sculpture, writing, cooking - make a list of all of the other creators you love and appreciate. Write down the artists and creators in your world who have meant something to you. They can be labels, bands, venues, writers or even people outside your discipline. Then *share your art with them*. No strings attached.

Don't send a demo to a label you love and say "Sign me.". Instead, send your music with a note, thanking them for what they do, for the records they released that got you through hard times, maybe even saved your life, and just let them know that you wanted to share your creation to say thank you.

Do that with everyone on your list. Organically, you will start to see things happen - conversations, messages, phone calls, other people sending you their own art, collaborations being arranged, new scenes forming, ongoing exchanges of art and ideas. Built into that will often be the thing you were after in the first place: a label wanting to release your record, another band wanting to play shows together, creators wanting to collaborate.

Even if nothing happens, you've done something positive and beautiful. You've helped bolster your creator community, made the scene stronger and potentially created new friendships. You've not only given your creation to people, but you've demonstrated your gratitude in the most beautiful way possible - by sharing something you created with other people who will likely do the same.

Absolutely continue to do all the things you already do - promotion, PR, socials, etc. Follow all the advice in this book, add this to the mix and see what happens.

Every little thing we can do to make our world of music a little more positive can only be a good thing.

Check out Andee's music at _aminorforest.com_ and _myheartaninvertedflame.com_

Music Publicity in 2021

Contributed by Ariel Hyatt

Publicity is valuable to you as an artist because it can help you get exposure. It gives you something to leverage within the industry and share on your socials, website and email list for extra traction and clout. In the minds of potential fans and listeners, it is always more believable when others say something about your music than when you say it yourself. Getting included in the media is essentially gaining a stamp of approval from music enthusiasts who take the time to curate music.

You probably want publicity because you would like to gain new listeners and fans. You may also be looking for name recognition and notoriety. Or perhaps you are deeply curious about what music media and tastemakers will say about your music. Maybe you think that if you get enough publicity, bigger and better things will happen for you. All of these reasons are valid.

However, keep some things in mind. Here's the first harrowing statistic when attempting to do your own publicity: 60,000 new tracks are released on Spotify every single day. Here's a second one: According to Muck Rack, there are six PR pros to every one journalist. In short, whether you want to hire a publicist or do it yourself, there's a lot of competition. And here is a third and very important thing to understand - the zeitgeist. Today, Chillwave, EDM, and Hip-Hop are much easier to work than smooth jazz and children's music due to the fact that there are more outlets available for "trendier" music.

Once a music blog or playlist begins to gain traction and solid social media numbers, hundreds of publicists, labels, managers, and artists all start vying for inclusion. In order to stand out from the masses, you have to have an understanding of how to communicate effectively, and you must also have a strategy. Music blogs and playlists frequently come and go. The reason for this is they are mostly created and run by fans who love music and are driven by passion. Sadly, passion doesn't pay the bills and over time, their enthusiasm wanes and the blogs and playlists shut down.

This means that as an artist, you must consistently cultivate new relationships with outlets as you release new music.

What A Music Publicist Does:

A music publicist's job is to liaise with the press. In other words, a publicist establishes working relationships between you and those in the media. As already outlined in this guide, media means blogs, playlists, and mostly online publications that are appropriate for you.

A publicist will save you a lot of time and work by leveraging their contacts and relationships. A strong publicist will be able to use these hard-won contacts to get you exposure that would otherwise take a lot of time to get on your own. The publicity that they place will help you establish your brand.

Your publicist will increase your name awareness to key media — music bloggers, podcasters, playlisters, music journalists, tastemakers — some of whom are more likely to pay attention to your music if a publicist they know and trust is introducing you.

Additionally, a publicist will get you legitimate press quotes to add to your arsenal to attract more industry attention from booking agents, managers, etc. You should also add these quotes to your website, socials and press kit. If they are strong, they will be with you for years to come.

A great publicist can make your life easier and accelerate your music career. However, you should not expect your publicist to get you a booking agent, live gigs, a label, or a publishing deal. A savvy and well-connected music publicist may be able to hook you up with other industry connections, but it is not in their job description.

Hiring a publicist should be like hiring another member of your band or adding a critical new member of your team, because that is exactly what you are doing. Everyone on your team has to be on the same page for you to advance. I advise you to choose someone you like and who is in alignment with your vision. You also want to make sure the publicist's contact base is right for your genre of music and that they shares in your short-term and long-term media goals.

We have all heard the phrase "all publicity is good publicity." It's beneficial to truly understand this and the truth is the average person remembers very little of what they read. They are not going to remember a lukewarm review or how large the playlist was that you were included in, only what was said or that you were included. A strong quote from the media or any playlist placement is beneficial no matter what outlet it comes from because the quotes and the plays that are generated are yours to keep forever and can never be taken away.

Find out more about Ariel at _arielhyatt.com_

ISRC Codes and Your Release

The International Standard Recording Code, known as the ISRC, is used to uniquely identify sound recordings. Whenever you release a song through a distributor, an ISRC will be generated. These are extremely important if you intend to release a song as a single, then also include it in an EP or album. In the following example, I refer to the single "Sick Boy'" from the Chainsmokers.

The Chainsmokers already have a huge following so naturally this song received millions of streams within its first two weeks of release. Here's the clever bit. A few weeks later, they released their next single "You Owe Me" as part of an EP with "Sick Boy". The EP was titled "Sick Boy... You Owe Me".

Since "Sick Boy" retained its original ISRC, the new EP appeared to instantaneously have millions of streams. In reality, these streams were attributed to "Sick Boy" alone. On the outside, however, the EP looked like an instant success.

They didn't stop there. A few weeks later, another single was released called "Everybody Hates Me" as a part yet another EP. This time, the EP included both prior releases - "Sick Boy" and "You Owe Me". Once again, on the first day, the release stream counts for this latest EP. This was all thanks to the ISRCs piecing everything together.

Aside from building up stream counts on a song through multiple releases, this is also a useful tool to build traction for an album. You can release a song every week or two weeks and give each song a chance to shine in Release Radar, Discover Weekly and other playlists, then give them another chance when the album is released. Look at other major artists like Diplo, Calvin Harris, Justin Timberlake. You can tell they have an album coming when you see multiple singles released in a calendar month.

While your fan base may not be as big as these artists, there is nothing stopping you to use these tactics while you grow your fan base.

Go to any streaming service and look at the top 10 songs for an artist. If you see one instance of a song in the top 10 and you know that artist has released that song multiple times (perhaps including a remaster) then it is likely to be the result of using the same ISRC.

On the flipside, if you see the same song multiple times in an artist's top 10 songs, it is likely they changed distributors and put the song out again not using the existing ISRC code. This means one song can show multiple times in your top 10, leaving less room for other songs.

To see how all this is applied, follow these links and notice that the stream count is merged across all three releases:

The Chainsmokers - Sick Boy

https://open.spotify.com/album/2QI0UclC8ipuXoyCva1C7K

The Chainsmokers - Sick Boy...You Owe Me

https://open.spotify.com/album/7ipPGzgSu86WmYyNyx2Kry

The Chainsmokers - Sick Boy...Everybody Hates Me

https://open.spotify.com/album/6Ok0x408eB6DmOrp13Llu3

Instant Gratification Tracks

Instant Gratification Tracks are individual tracks that are immediately available as part of a pre-order for an album. If you purchase an album as a pre-order, you may find that some of the tracks are available immediately to download or stream, before the album is available.

Artists can request to make tracks from an upcoming album available as Instant Gratification Tracks by asking their label or distributor. Currently this can only be done for iTunes/Apple Music, Amazon & Deezer.

Want to really give your fans an incentive to pre-order your album? You can set up to 49% of the total number of tracks as instant gratification tracks (for instance, a maximum of 5 out of a 12 tracks album).

In the above example, you can see that four tracks from the upcoming album are available to purchase and download immediately. These tracks can be purchased individually. If someone pre-orders the album they will also get those four tracks instantly.

Additionally, when making tracks available for Instant Gratification in iTunes, they will also be available to stream in Apple Music, as pictured below.

Piano Piano
Jeremiah Fraites
INSTRUMENTAL · PRE-RELEASE · JANUARY 22, 2021

▶ Play   ✕ Shuffle   + Add   ···

1. Departure
2. Dusty
▶ 3. Tokyo   +   1:16
4. Maggie   +   4:21
5. Nearsighted
6. Dreams
7. Possessed   +   1:43
8. An Air That Kills   +   3:23
9. Smreless Of Matters
10. Patromaniac
11. Arrival

11 SONGS, 38 MINUTES

Pre-Saves Are the New Pre-Order

Remember when pre-ordering an album from your favorite band meant visiting your local record store and leaving your name and phone number to secure a physical copy?

As the robots took over and technology advanced, people started purchasing their music digitally. This prompted the need for pre-orders to move from record stores to online. The benefit of a pre-order on iTunes, for example, was that people could pre-purchase your song, meaning that once the track was released, it would appear in the purchaser's library. The best part for an artist is that all of the pre-orders are counted on day 1. This means that all the "sales" over the weeks leading up to that release are all calculated on release day. This strategy is how many labels and artists have a "number 1 on iTunes on release day", even though the ranking falls in the days that follow.

With iTunes rumored to phase out downloads in the near future, it's time to plan ahead. This is where pre-saves come in.

A pre-save is usually delivered in the form of a gate (see Gates). It encourages fans to follow a simple action and in return be one of the first to hear an artist's new single. To set up a pre-save you will need the Spotify URI or Apple ID of the song. These can be received from your distributor sometimes 4 weeks in advance. Once you have these details, you can create a pre-save gate using one of the services mentioned in the Gates chapter.

Once the song is closer to release, you may be able to paste the URI in the Spotify search bar. You will be able to see the artwork and track title, though you won't be able to play the song until the official release date. Instead, you will see the songs grayed out. This is fine. The save button will still be available to click.

Fans can save your song to their Spotify library, meaning that as soon as your song goes live it is already in their saved section. This makes them feel warm and tingly knowing they can hear your song first. The other cool thing is that even though the songs are grayed out, users can still drag the song into their favorite playlists. As soon as the song goes live, it will already be in a bunch of your fans' playlists!

TIP: IN THE SPOTIFY DESKTOP APP, GO TO THE SETTINGS MENU AND SELECT "SHOW UNAVAILABLE SONGS IN PLAYLISTS". THIS WILL SHOW YOU SONGS THAT AREN'T LIVE YET (GRAYED OUT), SO YOU CAN SEE IF YOUR SONG HAS BEEN PLACED IN A PLAYLIST BEFORE RELEASE DAY. YOU CAN ALSO USE THIS AS A CURATOR TO DRAG A SONG INTO YOUR PLAYLIST IN THE DAYS BEFORE IT GOES LIVE. GO TO NEW MUSIC FRIDAY FOR ANOTHER COUNTRY THAT IS IN AN EARLIER TIMEZONE THAN YOURS, AND YOU WILL SEE THIS IN ACTION.

The Spotify Pre-Save: A Good Idea?

Contributed by Jay Gilbert

A Spotify pre-save is the modern equivalent to the pre-order.

Spotify doesn't officially offer the ability to pre-save music prior to release, but many platforms and distributors do. Is it a good idea? Yes and no.

When it's a good idea: When REAL fans click the pre-save link, it takes them to a landing page to save your upcoming music. On release day, the music is automatically added to their Spotify music libraries. In theory, this shows Spotify that there are users saving your music and hopefully playing it.

When it's NOT a good idea: When the users clicking the link and receiving the music on street date aren't going to listen to it.

Here's an example of the latter: You create a pre-save that says "Pre-save and you will automatically be entered into a contest for a signed guitar." Thousands of people enter for chance at the guitar. However, on street date, the music is added to their libraries and they don't listen to it. This shows Spotify that at worst, your fans aren't real, and at best, your fans aren't engaged.

It's not always about the number of plays, followers, listeners and playlists but the *right* ones.

‒ Encourage the RIGHT audience to engage and follow you on Spotify so your new music drops into their Discover Weekly and Release Radar playlists.

‒ Don't send anyone to Spotify or a pre-save link that won't LOVE your music

Find out more about Jay at label-logic.net

iTunes Is Still Here

iTunes isn't gone! It's just tucked away in the settings menu in the **Music** App. If you updated your Mac OS and found that iTunes mysteriously disappeared, here's where you can turn iTunes back on!

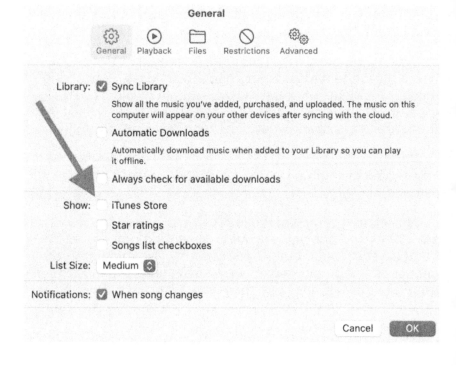

Going Far and Wide

Contributed by Jez Ryan

Often when I start working on a release campaign with an upcoming artist, I find they have this idea in their minds that they need to focus on their own country, city or even just their hometown. The idea of pitching their music to a worldwide audience is something they've not even considered at such an early stage of their development.

In my experience, I find it is very important to go far and wide with every release you do, especially for new and upcoming artists. Getting homegrown support is always great of course, especially when it comes to selling tickets for shows, but why just focus on such a small group of people when you have access to the entire world?

Pitching your music to a global market can potentially attract hundreds of thousands of streams on your song. Along with that, you should start to see a solid growth in your audience numbers as well.

After a few releases, you will then be able to see which territories are resonating with your music the most. Spotify for Artists is a good tool for this. Those demographics can then be used to better refine your social media campaigns to help maximize click-through rates and streaming results.

As your presence grows within the global music scene you might also start to attract international touring opportunities, which is far more beneficial to your project than just selling tickets at a few of your favorite venues back home. With that said, usually as your presence grows on a global scale it will also grow within your own territories. Before you know it you might even find yourself being invited to perform at some of the biggest venues in your local areas.

Find out more about Jez's work at _acidstag.com_ and _mammalsounds.com_

Influencer Marketing

From a quiet kid with a cool camera who takes great videos, to Dwayne "The Rock" Johnson, influencers can be anyone. An influencer can be someone with a large following, but more importantly, they have a collection of engaged followers who listen to what they have to say. Earlier in this book you were told to sign up with Instagram. If you have not yet done this, sign up now. I will wait.

Here's some homework. Go on Instagram, find some people who share your passion outside of music. If you like video games, search the hashtag #videogames and find someone with a large following and lots of engagement on their posts. Take the time to follow 20 of these influencers and write meaningful comments on their posts. I don't mean "nice video, I want to play that game". Be specific. Let's say they posted a video of them playing Grand Theft Auto V. Comment and say "Hey, I just finished the game with Trevor and found it was really tough, but I thought his ending was a much better story than the other two. Do you think he will return in the next GTA?". What you've done is show that you have paid attention to their video, made a thoughtful comment and asked for their opinion.

Now comes the exciting part, turn on notifications for Instagram and be ready. If they respond to your comment (you'll get notified because they will tag you in their reply), then respond immediately while they are active on the app and engaged. Your notification will be bumped to the top. If you are lucky enough to get another response, then ask them if you can send them a quick DM or email because you want to keep chatting and "don't want to get lost in the comments" or something along those lines.

Once you are in the DM, don't talk about yourself, just keep engaging them and asking great questions. This is developing the relationship. If you play it cool, you may find they follow you back (which is why it's important to never be fake in your social media profiles). After they follow you back, it's time to ask them a little more about themselves, such as

"How long have you been a gamer?" or "Do you have other hobbies you enjoy?".

Once they respond, you will likely get a response followed by "...How about yourself?". Now is when you tell them in two sentences what you are about. "Avid gamer from California, loved Nintendo but I'm now all about PS4. Also make electronic music and dream to have a song featured in a video game" works. Once you've let them know that you also create music, you've given them the opportunity to respond if they are interested.

Now, be careful. It's still possible to scare them off. If they ask to hear some of your music, don't send them multiple links and DMs. Breathe and pick your best song that represents your sound. Tell them a little about the track you send them so they know what to prepare for. "It's a deep electronic chill track that reminds me of driving home after a long day".

Now leave them to listen. If you haven't heard from them, but see they have posted new content online, it would be good to comment on the next post, without mentioning your music.

There is a good chance that if you give them enough time and then follow up (say 2 weeks), they will think you are chill and be more likely to respond. If they show any interest in your music, here's the cool part. Tell them that you would be happy to send them a copy of your song to use for free in any of their videos. This also means that you now have a chance to get your music in front of their audience.

If they bite, be sure to send links to your social media with an easy download link (Dropbox or Google Drive). This gives them everything they need. You will most likely see your artist and song title in the video description as well as perhaps a tag in the comments and a link to your socials (which is why short links are important because Instagram doesn't allow clickable links). In other words, people only see the text version (e.g. johnsmithmusic.com or bit.ly/johnsmithmusic). Neither is clickable but people are likely to remember and type the text into their web browser.

Experiences

Contributed by Jay Gilbert

A great new revenue stream has emerged, ignited by services like Cameo, Thrillz.co.uk, Patreon, Twitch, and OnlyFans.

Making a sustainable career from solely music sales / streams / downloads may not be a smart strategy today. Streaming is not the enemy, but a stream isn't monetarily worth the same as a download. A download isn't worth the same as a CD and a CD isn't worth the same as a vinyl LP.

Sync licensing, touring and merch can also generate significant revenue. But so can "experiences."

What are experiences?

- Paid meet & greets

- Personal audio / video messages

- Exclusive access

- Recording / writing with your favorite artist

- House concerts

- Personalized / signed merch and handwritten lyrics

There's tons of potential here. During the pandemic, The Accidentals offered hand-knitted scarves and D&D sessions. The Lickerish Quartet still offer music lessons, writing sessions and even record shopping and dinner with the band!

Get creative. Offer your fans something no one else can.

Find out more about Jay's work at _label-logic.net_

Is It A Good Playlist?

With so much focus and energy put towards getting on a playlist, there's also an ongoing concern about whether a playlist is actually going to help or hinder an artist. Here's a couple of ways to see if a playlist is delivering listeners.

Please note that there is no way of knowing who these listeners are exactly so this information is best to be treated as general information.

Spotify - Discovered On

Go to an artist profile and scroll down to the Discovered On section. This will show the playlists that are delivering the highest number of listeners. It will not show the number of listeners, but this is a good guide on which playlists are delivering the most for that artist.

Click **See All**, and you can currently see up to the top 50 playlists delivering monthly listeners on Spotify. This is available in the web app by going to open.spotify.com in your web browser and looking at an artist profile then scrolling down to the Discovered On section.

Deezer - Playlists Section

Deezer shows up to the top 100 playlists that are delivering listeners for an artist. For example, popular EDM artist Marshmello has a large number of playlist adds on Deezer. The top 100 can be seen by going to his artist profile and looking at the Playlists section or by going to this direct link:

https://www.deezer.com/en/artist/7890702/related_playlist

Playlists >

New Dance
50 tracks - 277,294 fans

Fresh House
50 tracks - 24,161 fans

Pulse
50 tracks - 257,485 fans

SEE MORE PLAYLISTS

Isitagoodplaylist.Com

Here's a really helpful tool:

isitagoodplaylist.com

You can paste in the link to any Spotify playlist and it will cross reference both the songs featured in the playlist with the artist's "Discovered On" analytics to determine how well a playlist is delivering. It's free and doesn't require any account creation.

Check Your Stats

If you have been added to a playlist, you will be able to see streams and listeners for that playlist by logging into your artist tools (e.g. Apple Music for Artists or Spotify for Artists). This is a great way to see how much that playlist is driving listeners and streams.

Is The Playlist Well Curated?

Listen to the playlist first. Do you enjoy listening? Is it well curated and something you would let play, or is it so poorly curated that you want to skip? If you don't find enjoyment from the playlist, it's safe to safe others may not either.

Curators: You may think that by placing someone's song on your playlist you are helping them, but that may not always be the case. If you have a chilled out study beats playlist and you put an upbeat electronic song in the middle of that playlist, you may get some listeners for that artist, but most listeners may skip that song. This will impact both that artist and related artists. It can actually hurt the others long-term.

Twitter Follower Hack

Simply using a different share link can show a prompt for users to follow you on Twitter.

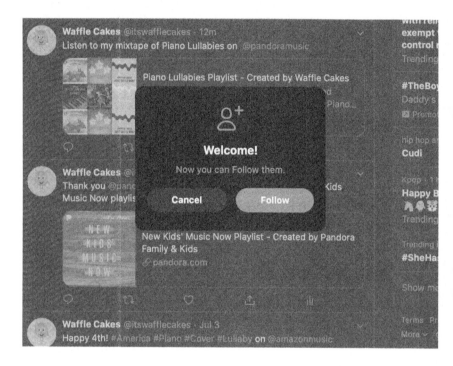

Here's how to do this. Take the below URL and replace **USERNAME** with your Twitter username.

https://twitter.com/intent/user?screen_name=**USERNAME**

For example, if @itswafflecakes is the Twitter username, delete the @ and use the below URL.

https://twitter.com/intent/user?
screen_name=itswafflecakes

When people click it, they will now be served a popup with one of two options - **Cancel** or **Follow**. Hopefully, the ease of clicking through will mean more followers for you by using this simple method.

YouTube Follower Hack

This is a very simple hack to encourage new visitors to subscribe to your YouTube channel via a popup. Keep in mind that clicking Subscribe takes the same amount of energy as closing out the popup. While not everyone may subscribe when prompted, making it easier for them will give you a better chance.

To create a link, you simply need to take an existing YouTube URL such aa:

http://www.youtube.com/askmikewarner

Now simply add ?sub_confirmation=1 to the end of the URL:.

http://www.youtube.com/askmikewarner?sub_confirmation =1

You've most likely subscribed to your YouTube channel already, which means if you test the follow URL with ? sub_confirmation=1 included the popup will not show. You can get past this by opening a private tab in your web browser and then entering the URL. If this doesn't work, you can unsubscribe to your channel and then test the link to see the Subscribe popup.

Anywhere you share your link to your YouTube channel, you can use the full URL to grow your followers. Add it to your website, email signature, social media posts and profiles. Every time you share the link to your channel use this new URL instead.

If the new URL is a little long remember you can use a URL shortener.

The Facebook Birthday Post

I can't take credit for being the first to think of this but it's too brilliant not to share. This can be applied to promote a playlist, new song or to get some follows on a new artist profile.

If you have a birthday coming up on Facebook (don't be cheeky and change it), then follow these steps.

Go to **Privacy Settings, Timeline** and **Tagging**, and change "Who can post on your timeline?" to "Only me".

Post a new profile photo with a great shot of yourself. In the photo description, mention how amazing it would be if everyone followed your new playlist, saved your new single or followed your artist profile. People will be notified of your birthday a few days in advance, so post early. Remember that some of your friends may be located elsewhere in the world in different timezones.

On the day of, Facebook will notify all your friends that it is your birthday. When they go to post on your wall, there will be no option to do a new post so they will comment on your most recent post. In this case, it will be your new profile photo.

All of these comments and likes on your new photo will generate high engagement with your post, meaning it will appear in more of your friends' news feeds. Keep in mind that your Facebook profile is about you, a real person, so try to include a story with the photo to make it more interesting. Use a photo of you on a hike, for example, with the description "Feeling on top of the world here at X mountain and super excited to now have my music on X, follow me here [link]." If you are feeling extra clever, use a short link.

Keep Selling CDs

CDs are an additional revenue stream. I compare it to the feeling of going into a store and buying a product. It makes you feel good. Fans like me go to a show or buy CDs for this reason. They may never listen to or even unwrap the CD, but the purchase part of the process felt good knowing that the money went to the artist.

What usually happens next is the fan gets in their car and then starts streaming that very same album via a streaming service. The artist now has revenue from the CD sale (let's say $5 profit per CD) as well as from the streaming service.

I definitely don't recommend just handing out CDs for free to everyone you meet as it can cause people to not see value in your music. If someone pays for something, even a few dollars, they are more likely to make time to listen or at least keep it in their car, on their bookshelf etc. That CD may one day be passed on to a friend with a "listen to this" comment. That's word-of-mouth marketing.

Want to increase the value of your CD? Make sure you sign it for the fan. If there is a personal message with their name on it, it's safe to assume they will keep it around. They may even take a photo and share it on social media.

When looking at CD manufacturers, keep in mind that size matters. If you use full size jewel cases for your CDs, the price of postage will increase. There's also the risk of the case being cracked during transit, and it doesn't really fit into a jacket pocket or purse as easily.

I suggest looking at thin cardboard sleeves. Some distributors call these eco packs which, as the name suggests, are also good for the environment. Fans will be more likely to purchase these if they easily fit in their pocket.

Say Thank You

This may seem like an odd thing to mention, but always say thank you. It takes less than one second to say and can be the difference between someone feeling happy with their decision to support you, or feel like they were not important enough to be thanked and their support wasn't valued. You will most likely not hear from them again.

If someone really helps you early in your career, don't ever forget them. Find a way to thank them. I have a friend who runs a large independent playlist network. He helped me immensely both through supporting my music and with advice when it came to building my own playlists.

It started as a thank you, then led to me booking a flight when he was speaking at a conference in another city. I shouted him a few beers. ("Shouting" means buying in Australia.) Years later, and we are now good friends and still share music and tips. That man's name is Carlos, and he is the founder of Indiemono, one of the largest independent playlist brands on Spotify with over 3.5 million followers across all of their playlists.

So, always say thank you. Remember those who supported you from the start. You never know where they may be in a few years time. If one of you grows, you both grow. That, and being grateful should hopefully come naturally.

Here's some suggestions for different ways to say thank you:

— Share the playlist as your Artist Pick on your Spotify profile. You can do this at artists.spotify.com

— Tweet and tag the curator, telling everyone to go check out their playlist

— Post a brief video of you in the studio thanking the curator for adding your song.

TIP: IF YOU TAKE A SCREENSHOT OF A CURATORS PLAYLIST, BE SURE TO CLICK "FOLLOW" FIRST SO IT SHOWS THAT YOU ARE FOLLOWING AND LISTENING TO THEIR PLAYLIST. THIS MAKES THE "THANK YOU" MORE GENUINE AND WILL LIKELY RECEIVE A MORE POSITIVE RESPONSE FROM THE CURATOR.

The Power of Community

Contributed by Dr. Sue Oreszczyn, FRSA:

What you do is not done in isolation. Community is both important and powerful. You can create one around what you do and also tapping into existing ones. You can develop a fan community and also an artist and/or playlist community.

A supportive community is also good for mental health, especially in an industry where critique and rejection are inevitable from time to time. It can, however, be difficult to build your own from scratch. Fortunately, there are an increasing number of mutually supportive music communities - locally and on social media platforms - that can be tapped into. These communities are often very welcoming to newcomers. If they are online, they may include not just playlist creators and artists but also radio or YouTube presenters, bloggers, independent record labels and promoters etc.

Online music communities tend to grow organically, so it's good to watch out for them and join those that appear suitable, welcoming, supportive and fun. It's a great way to get to know others in the music industry and tap into the experience and knowledge of others. For example, on Twitter artists can be found supporting fellow artists by sharing new music across fan bases, sharing playlists and useful information etc. Online communities are also often connected to physical communities, so while joining one may result in a wider fan base, DSP playlist placements, radio show plays, reviews etc., it can also lead to invitations to play at live gigs.

Find out more about Sue's work at grassrootsmusicnetwork.org

Find More Curators

Now that you are starting to make some strong connections with curators, the next step is to find ways to connect with others through them, sometimes it is as simple as asking nicely. With these examples, it is important to put your own touch on the conversations / emails.

Ask For An Introduction

Once you have built rapport and have a curator that you speak with a few times per month, it's ok to ask them the following question. I've even drafted an example for you:

"Hi [NAME], it's been a pleasure sharing music with you these last few months, and I'm so happy to be able to support your music as well. I was wondering if you have any other contacts that would be interested in a similar type of arrangement? I'd be happy to introduce you to some of my contacts in return, as I am sure we can help each other through facilitated introductions"

In this email I have explained why I am asking for other contacts (because I know the value of a larger network), while also offering an introduction to my contacts (something of value in return).

If you are asked to introduce one of your contacts, ask them directly first to make sure they are ok with this. You don't want to upset your existing contacts who are already happily sharing music with you.

What If A Curator Leaves Their Job?

If you have developed a relationship with a curator and they have advised that they are leaving their job, you should follow these steps:

Make yourself aware of the circumstances, if they are leaving their record label job to pursue their music career you can assume they are leaving on good terms.

Wish them all the best, and ask if you can keep in touch as you'd love to hear about their next moves. You never know - They could move on to a bigger role in a similar company and you'll be glad they gave you their personal email/cell.

Once they have acknowledged your well wishes and shown they are happy to keep in touch, you can ask them if it's possible to be introduced to their successor as you would love to continue sharing music with them as well.

There is nothing more valuable than a personal introduction, especially when it is from the previous staff member. It's like meeting a friend of a friend. There is instantly a level of comfort and trust involved. It's on you to build it from there.

Tip: When engagement with a contact is at its peak (or after you have exchanged more than a couple of nice emails), it is a good time to connect on LinkedIn. A connection request on LinkedIn is far less invasive and more accepted in the early stage of a new relationship with a curator. The best part about requesting a new connection on LinkedIn is that you will be notified if they move on to another role or get promoted. The platform is also a great way to continue reaching them via messaging.

Out Of Office Responses

This is the next best thing to an introduction. Let's say you email your playlist curator at record label X and you receive an out-of-office response. There's little chance they are going to reply or place your song, but there is a very high chance they will include an alternative contact to reach out to in their absence.

This is the perfect time to do a self introduction. Here's an example of how I would reach out. Please rewrite this in your own words.

"Hello [NAME],

I usually share new music with John, and I know that he is currently on holiday in Hawaii (1), which I am extremely jealous of. I was told that you may be the best person to contact in his absence and just wanted to reach out as I have new music to share if possible? (2)

If you are not the best contact for this, can you please point me towards them and I will be sure to spare your inbox from my musical pitches. (3)

All the best, Michael"

It's important that I know John, and well enough to know that he is on holiday in Hawaii. This will likely cause the recipient to keep reading.

I didn't pitch in the email. I asked for permission, which is very important because if this email goes to the wrong person and there is a bunch of song links they are likely to just move it to the "I don't have time for this" basket.

Lastly, I gave them an opportunity to push me towards someone else - another contact, maybe a better contact for what I am looking for.

If they respond positively, hit them with your song pitch and use a little charm. If all goes well, you may just have another contact at that record label.

If they respond with another contact, you should reach out to them following the process again and explaining how you were connected.

Work Hard Podcast Hard

It's not uncommon for artists to also have a podcast. Some of us use it as a way to show other passions. Whatever your reason, I wanted to share this quick summary of where you can go to make sure your podcast is available in as many places as possible.

Listeners will use their app or service of choice, so don't miss out on potential listeners thinking you need to be exclusive to one platform. Unless someone offers you a highly lucrative deal to provide a podcast exclusively, there's no need to only use one.

I submitted my podcast to all of these services successfully and (shameless plug) you can check it out at WorkHardPlaylistHard.com/p/podcast.

Podcast Submission Links

Amazon Music https://podcasters.amazon.com

Audible https://podcasters.amazon.com

Apple Podcasts: https://podcastsconnect.apple.com

Breaker: https://www.breaker.audio/i/upstream

Deezer: https://podcasters.deezer.com

Google Podcast: https://search.google.com/search-console/welcome

iHeart Radio: https://www.iheart.com/content/submit-your-podcast

JioSaavn https://yourcast.jiosaavn.com

Pandora: https://amp.pandora.com/podcasts

Radio Public: https://podcasters.radiopublic.com

Spotify: https://podcasters.spotify.com

Stitcher: https://www.stitcher.com/content-providers.php

TuneIn: https://help.tunein.com/contact/add-podcast-S19TR3Sdf

Distribution

I use Anchor to distribute my podcast. They do a great job, but I found that by grabbing the RSS feed from Anchor in the Settings menu, I was able to also add my podcast to the above services This makes my program reachable to an even wider audience, which is important to getting my message out and increasing the reach for my guests.

There are also numerous other paid and free podcast services. Anchor was the right fit for me, but always do your own research to find the best solution for you.

Social Media Posts

I use Headliner to create audiograms, which are social media-ready visualizers with images with transcriptions of the speech and a synced waveform. Headliner has a free option which I've found more than sufficient. I then upload these visualizers to my Facebook page, Instagram and YouTube channels.

Payola Vs. Playola

Contributed by Jay Gilbert

"PAYOLA" vs "PLAYOLA"

Let's not mince words. Both are simply wrong and bad for the music industry. One is illegal.

"Payola" is the act of paying for radio airplay without disclosing that the play was for pay. It's against US federal law. US airwaves are publicly owned and regulated by the FCC.

"Playola" is the act of paying for placement in playlists on digital service providers like Spotify and Apple Music. While this may be unethical and is certainly against DSP terms of service, it's not illegal (yet).

DSP playlists can be broken down into two groups; User-curated and DSP-curated. If I create a playlist, it's user-curated. If Spotify creates a playlist, it's DSP-curated.

There are also commercial services (as mentioned in prior chapters) that have networks of user curators who will listen to submissions, give feedback and sometimes even add songs to their playlists. This is not considered payola as they are being compensated for their feedback and playlist adds are not guaranteed.

While everyone likes a quick win, please do your research. Follow the tips in previous chapters to give your music the best chance to shine, both long and short term.

Find out more about Jay's work at _label-logic.net_

Final Thoughts

This book has been a long time coming. I really wanted to share everything I wish I knew when I started out. I hope it helps you.

The industry is changing constantly, and I'm always learning. *Work Hard Playlist Hard* will continue to be updated and revised, and I will continue to share even more knowledge in the future.

Since the first release in 2018, this book has already been updated countless times. A lot has changed in the music streaming world. A lot has changed for me as well. This book has opened doors for me to participate in conference panels, host live workshops, appear on various podcasts and even appear in my first live TV interview on CNBC.

None of this would have been possible if it wasn't for the amazing support I have received. Whether it was a tweet, email or even just telling a friend, thank you. I feel a huge level of responsibility to make sure I continue delivering current and reliable information to help further your career.

The music industry is an ever-evolving landscape. As this is now the second edition of the book, please don't hold back if there's something you would like me to add, expand or update in a future edition.

In the meantime, go out there, keep creating, keep learning and keep sharing.

Thanks for reading.

Mike Warner

@askmikewarner
WorkHardPlaylistHard.com

Credits

Second edition edited by Erica Young

First edition edited by Dr. Sue Oreszczyn, FRSA and Ranya Khoury

Cover art created by Spectator Jonze

Words by Mike Warner

Guest Contributors: Andee Connors, Ariel Hyatt, Bree Noble, Cheryl B. Engelhardt, Chris Robley, Jay Gilbert, Jari Kurkaa, Jez Ryan, Karen Allen, Kelli-Leigh, LUK, Mark Tavern, Nick Ditri, Nina Las Vegas, Ryden, Spectator Jonze, Sue Oresczyn, Troy Carter Jr and Uberjak'd

Thank You

This book would not be possible without the support, patience, love and encouragement I've received from so many of you. To my beautiful wife, my parents, my sister, family, friends, colleagues, artists, pets and everyone I've had the pleasure of connecting with, thank you from the bottom of my heart.

To think that this book almost never happened is scary. Self doubt is real, and so is imposter syndrome. Yet here we are - bigger and better!

Thank you for picking this book up, investing time in yourself and sharing what you've learned to help others. You are appreciated.

Thanks Erica for being the glue that kept WHPH together when I needed to take some time offline in early 2020. It would not exist without your encouragement, dedication and spirit. You are so greatly appreciated and go above and beyond!

Thanks to all of the incredible contributors that shared their time, knowledge and feedback. This book is going to help a lot of people. It wouldn't be the same without your contributions.

Thanks to all the fantastic people that booked me to speak, welcomed me into their office, classroom, computer screen, TV screen, book store and conference room. There are so many more to thank that I would need to extend this book. I'll be sure to do it directly.

More Learning

Here are other books I have read and recommend.

Books

- How to Make It In The New Music Business by Ari Herstand

- The Slotify Method by George Goodrich

- All You Need to Know About the Music Business by Donald Passman

- Twitch for Musicians by Karen Allen

- The Musician's Profit Path by Bree Noble

- $150,000 Music Degree by Rick Barker and Wade Sutton

- The Ultimate Guide to Music Publicity by Ariel Hyatt

- The Independent Music Sector by Neil March

- Get Verified on Instagram with Under 5,000 Followers by Call Me Ace

- The Plain & Simple Guide To Music Publishing by Randall D. Wixen

Courses

I have created a number of courses available at WorkHardPlaylistHard.com, including "Introduction to Playlists" and "Artists Profiles and Tools". You may find some overlap with the content in this book, but if video walkthroughs are your thing, feel free to check them out.

Affiliate Programs

Why not make some extra cash recommending products you genuinely believe in while you build a following? For instance, If you found value from this book, wouldn't you naturally refer it to your friends and peers anyway?

You can use affiliate links from major retailers to share links to almost any product and receive commission for sales you generate. Here are a few programs you can sign up with. You can share links to the Work Hard Playlist Hard book, or even Work Hard Playlist Hard merchandise on Amazon. Additionally, you can share links to any music on Apple Music and make commission if someone subscribes.

Here's some affiliate programs I currently participate in.

Amazon Affiliate

Apple Affiliate

Barnes & Noble Affiliate

Testimonials

"My friend Mike is my go-to for streaming advice, mainly because he comes from music and the music I like. He has that special touch and feel for where a track can work well, not just a statistics type knowledge. His playlists are always put together in an organic way - not just strategically - and they are solid musically. I have seen him grow from one playlist to a massive operation over the years."

StoneBridge (Grammy nominated producer and remixer)

"I have followed Mike since the early days of Spotify, when creating public playlists on streaming services was something new and exciting. A number of independent curators began curating and sharing Spotify playlists out of a strong desire to help and support new and emerging independent artists. Unknown artists would be slipped in alongside better known artists in a bid to give them a voice. Mike was one of these curators. I spotted him early on as a result of his integrity, kindness and willingness to help others. As he learned for himself, he freely shared his knowledge of a rapidly evolving and often bewildering music industry with others. Fortunately, he continues to do so today. Mike is both knowledgeable and one of the good guys, and his book reflects this."

Dr Sue Oreszczyn FRSA (Academic and founding member of the Grassroots Music Network)

"Mike knows the streaming world extremely well and as an artist has a unique view on the sector too. With a proven track record of success, this book is a must read for anyone interested in this space."

Kieron Donoghue (Founder of Humble Angel Records)

"What impresses me most about Mike is that his knowledge of the digital music world is born from a true love for music (unfortunately not always the case in the biz these days). From both an artist and industry perspective, Mike always seems to be up on the trends and is always looking to find new ways to expose not only his groups music, but the music of other talented artists from around the world to wider audiences. Beyond his clear expertise in the areas that he works, he also just happens to be a great person to deal with, talk to and collaborate with. Nothing but respect for his hustle and know how."

Brian Delaney (Tommy Boy Records)

"It still amazes me how much Mike knows about the streaming world, although it makes complete sense. He's constantly looking for new endeavors to expand his knowledge about the digital music sector. Whether it's curating a playlist network, growing his own artist profile, recording informational podcasts or speaking at conferences Mike clearly has a keen eye for all things music. Over a few months' time, I've been able to watch his own projects grow substantially, showcasing his ability to provide top-notch advice that holds value."

Ranya Khoury (Spinnin Records)

Music Industry Glossary

Here is a bonus section of commonly used terms in the streaming world today. While not every term below is mentioned in this book, I hope it helps you navigate the music industry a bit more easily.

A/B Testing: A/B testing is a way of identifying which of two options is more effective. It involves presenting a sample group of users with two versions of a single variable - like two different designs of the same webpage - and measuring which option, A or B, gets better results.

A&R (Artist & Repertoire): A&Rs are in charge of talent scouting and overseeing artistic development of recording artists and songwriters. They also listen to demos and will usually oversee negotiations between record labels and an artist.

Analytics: Analytics are simply the information gleaned from data or statistics, like the number of song streams or how many new users followed your artist page in a given period. These numbers offer insight into what strategies are working best for you.

AQH (Average Quarter Hour): This is the average number of listeners in a fifteen minute period. Mostly related to radio.

Asset: Assets, or creative, are the media you have or will create specifically to promote a release, including music videos, promotional photos and album artwork.

Attribution: Attribution measures the effectiveness different marketing strategies, tracking which lead to a conversion and allowing you to see where your campaign is most successful.

Campaign: A campaign is the entire overview of the marketing push behind a release or tour, or even an effort to increase public awareness of you as an artist. It includes your strategies, assets, release dates, analytics, budget, and more.

Content: Content is the broad swath of media or information you share with the public, including songs, videos, blog posts, tweets and off-the-cuff Instagram stories.

Conversion: A conversion is when a user performs a desired behavior such as clicking through a link and then purchasing something, following your profile or listening to a song. Conversion rate, similar to CTR, measures how often this happens versus how many people see your content.

CPC (Cost Per Click): The average cost paid per click when running a digital marketing campaign.

CPM (Cost Per Mile): The cost per thousand impressions in a digital marketing campaign.

Creative: Creative, or assets, are the media you create specifically to promote a release, including music videos, promotional photos and album artwork.

Cross-Platform: This refers to viability across multiple platforms like social media pages, or mobile and desktop interfaces. Aided by analytics, a cross-platform strategy leverages the specific benefits of each medium.

CTA (Call To Action): A call to action is a prompt that asks a user to complete a desired behavior as determined by you, like streaming a single or buying an album. It can be as simple as "Click here" or "Listen now".

CTR (Click-Through Rate): Click-through rate, or CTR, is the number of times something is clicked on versus the times a viewer was shown the asset, whether it's an ad, song or link to a merch store.

Curator: A person that manages a playlist or station, adding and removing music.

DAW (Digital Audio Workstation): A digital audio workstation (DAW) is an electronic device or music production software used for recording, editing and producing audio files. Some popular DAWss are Ableton Live, Logic and Pro Tools.

Distribution: Distribution is what makes your music available to stores and streaming services. This can go through a label or a third-party company, like CD Baby, DistroKid or TuneCore.

DJ (Disc Jockey): A person who plays recorded music using equipment. They are in control of the music. Examples include a radio jockey and a turntablist.

DM (Direct Message): Commonly referred to when speaking about social media. People can send a direct message in Facebook, Instagram and Twitter, for example.

DSP (Digital Service Provider): A DSP is a digital store such as iTunes, or a streaming platform such as Spotify. Please note that in audio, DSP can also mean Digital Signal Processing (see next).

DSP (Digital Signal Processing): This is how digital signals are manipulated and changed.

EAN (European Article Number): An (EAN) is the European version of a UPC. Every release will have an EAN assigned.

EP (Extended Play): An EP is a release that has between 2-7 tracks. These releases are shorter than albums.

FOH (Front Of House): Front Of House is the part of a performance venue that is open to the public, such as auditorium and foyers.

ID3 Tag: These tags can be found on MP3 or similar audio files. They contain information such as the artist's name, song title, album name and genre.

IP (Intellectual Property): This refers to creations such as inventions, designs, symbols, literary and artistic works, plus names and images used in commerce. Find out more about IP on the World Intellectual Property Organization Website at wipo.int/about-ip.

ISRC (International Standard Recording Code): Every track has an unique ISRC encoded. An ISRC is a 12-character, alphanumeric code which acts like a barcode, helping collection societies and streaming platforms know that your song was played.

ISWC (International Standard Musical Work Code): An ISWC is an 11-character alphanumeric code usually assigned by a collection society. It tracks the song title, songwriter(s), music publisher(s) and corresponding ownership shares.

KPI: A KPI (Key Performance Indicator) is the numeric goal you set for any facet of your campaign. This can be a certain amount of streams, album sales, shows booked, etc. that you want to achieve through marketing.

LD (Lighting Director): Oversees all lighting and visual effects for performances

LP (Long Play): An LP is a release that contains 8 or more tracks. This comes from "long play vinyl record" and now is a way to identify a full-length album.

Lift: Lift is the amount of improvement that results from a new campaign. By comparing the analytics of those who receive your new marketing strategy versus those who still experience your old plan, you can see where you've improved or declined.

Muzak: A type of background music that is played in retail stores and other public establishments.

OAC: Official Artist Channel. Many DSPs allow artists to claim their artist channel, sometimes indicated by a blue tick.

Organic Vs. Paid: Organic marketing, or "inbound marketing," involves content that's created naturally by an artist, like blog posts or social media updates. It can be optimized to reach bigger audiences using tactics like search engine optimization (SEO). Paid marketing is a premium strategy, like advertising, promoting posts or doing sponsored content. By investing in this, you can potentially reach more listeners and turn them into customers more quickly.

OTB (Out Of The Box): The acronym for "Out Of The Box" — any production work that is done on external equipment outside of a computer, such as an analogue mixer, or using hardware FX units.

Pitch: A pitch is you, your publicist, manager, or booking agent trying to sell another party on an idea. The goal might be getting your music written up by a publication, earning brand sponsorships, finding venues to book you, or pitching your music for playlist consideration. A well-targeted pitch can land you many opportunities.

Press / Media Release: A press release is a statement that alerts the media to what you're up to — a new release, tour, collaboration, etc.— in the hopes it will get coverage.

PRO (Performing Rights Organization): A local organization that helps artists collect royalties for songs played in public venues like bars, nightclubs, restaurants, radio stations, music festivals and retail stores.

PUGC (Professional User Generated Content): User generated content that is managed by a marketing team that handles business collaborations and product placements.

Reach: Reach is the total number of unique users who are exposed to your content. It can help you understand how effective advertising on a specific platform is.

SPI (Spotify Popularity Index): A ranking number from 0-100. 100 is the highest possible level of popularity attainable on Spotify.

Targeting: Targeting is a way of narrowing down your desired audience into certain demographics and using that information to figure how out to best reach them, like promoting your music on a social network they're most likely to use.

TM (Tour Manager): A manager that travels with the artists, making sure all accommodations, transportation, finances are organized and handling communications related to the tour.

Touring Market: A touring market is the geographical and demographical areas in which you plan to perform. This can be broad, like "Europe," or specific, such as "towns with populations under 50,000 across the Midwest US." Part of your campaign will involve determining how to target fans in these markets.

UGC (User Generated Content): Anything made by a user, such as a TikTok video or other social media post.

UPC (Universal Product Code): A UPC code is used for tracking products in stores. Every release will have a UPC assigned. UPC codes are used in the US and Canada.

About the Author

Australian-born Mike Warner is one of the leading experts on the world of streaming music. Mike's multifaceted roles as both a freelance label consultant and Director of Artist Relations at Chartmetric have allowed him to develop and execute strategic digital campaigns for both major and independent clients.

Now a best-selling author as well as a public speaker, Mike has shared his insights on every stage, from guest starring on numerous podcasts and appearing live on CNBC to speaking at the music industry's largest conferences including SXSW, NAMM and ADE.

Based on the success of the first edition of *Work Hard Playlist Hard*, Mike has expanded the world of WHPH into a full online educational portal workhardplaylisthard.com and a podcast series *Streamline With Mike Warner*.

An independent artist himself, Mike understands the challenges facing artists today better than anyone. A bit of a rebel and an obstinate supporter of independent artists, Mike continues to be unrelentingly passionate about empowering musicians with the tools they need to succeed.

As an educator, author, speaker, executive and leader, Mike's work has gained him recognition among his peers as the go-to authority on the forefront of the digital music world.

For all things streaming, ask Mike Warner.

Printed in Great Britain
by Amazon

66335522R00132